Learning the Basics of New Testament Greek

Student Workbook

LEARNING THE BASICS OF NEW TESTAMENT GREEK

Student Workbook

By
George Aristotle Hadjiantoniou Ph.D.

Compiled by P. J. Bell
Revised and Edited by James H. Gee

AMG
PUBLISHERS
Chattanooga, TN 37422

Learning the Basics of New Testament Greek (Student Workbook Edition)

ISBN 0-89957-802-0

Printed in the United States of America
04 03 02 01 00 99 –R– 6 5 4 3 2 1

Acknowledgements

This edition of George Hadjiantoniou's Greek Workbook has gone through a major revision process since the original printing in 1985. Much of this revision work has been done by Dr. James H. Gee, a volunteer editor here at AMG Publishers, with the assistance of Dr. Dennis Wisdom, a long-time professor of New Testament Greek. Dr. Gee is a brilliant Greek scholar and professor, and without his dedication and tireless effort, this revised edition would not have been possible. Other valuable staff members and volunteers have had a hand in this project, and we at AMG Publishers are grateful for them. These people include: Anne Arnett, Dr. Warren Baker, Tony Cortman, Symeon Ioannidis, and Rick Steele, Jr.

Although Dr. Hadjiantoniou and these fine scholars have labored meticulously to make this work free from error, they are not infallible. If you should find a mistake, please let us know.

NOTE: All parenthetical references such as (**3 § 6, i**) should be interpreted in the following order:
(lesson number § paragraph number, roman numeral subpoint)

—THE EDITORS

Table of Contents

LEARNING THE BASICS OF NEW TESTAMENT GREEK STUDENT WORKBOOK

Preface

TO THE STUDENT OF NEW TESTAMENT GREEK: This is your workbook. It will help you to understand the Greek language so that you will have greater knowledge of the Word of God. May this give you insight into the truths that were written to us by Christians of the New Testament era.

It is suggested that the student read the chapter in the textbook and then read the corresponding chapter in this workbook, without attempting to fill in the blanks. The student should then go back to the textbook and read the chapter a second time, giving special attention to those sections of the chapter where he was unsure of his answers.

When you make any mistakes, go back to the textbook and review the chapter to determine the reason for your incorrect answer. Then proceed to the next chapter, repeating the same method.

The breathing marks and the accents are to be learned along with the spelling of the words.

SECTION I

This section contains exercises based on Lessons 1-40 in your textbook. You will find that learning Greek involves quite a bit of writing. You may have trouble memorizing certain words, so utilize mnemonic devices to help your memory. Associate difficult words with familiar objects or other similar words. With practice, these memory aids will become unnecessary, but they will be helpful, even necessary, in the beginning.

SECTION II

The vocabulary listed in the back of the workbook will aid you in memorizing words from the textbook. The Summary of Morphology pages (pp. 259-270 in the textbook) are not in the workbook. Do not hesitate to use aids available to you. Your own study methods will be most helpful. In addition, you may try writing words on file cards, making charts, drawing pictures, or any other materials that will give you a visual aid to make the learning process easier.

Section I

The work sheets in this section contain information from lessons in the textbook. These will help you to understand the Greek grammar of the New Testament more quickly. It is necessary to follow the textbook closely, because only portions of the lessons are emphasized. There are sentences to complete, lists, etc., for each lesson. Occasionally there are other aids, so look for them. The first section will include grammar, syntax, and words from previous lessons. The word lists in Section II will be helpful. Get a good foundation, and the process of learning will be easier. Remember, however, that no teaching method can take the place of study and perseverance.

Lesson 1

1. The Greek Language dates back to the conquests of _____ the
_____. Of the original Greek dialect, the _____ Greek became the literary language of Greece.

Common communication first developed among the _____ of Alexander's _____ who followed them. "_____" means "common." It later acquired a (broader/lesser) meaning. The second name of the New Testament Greek language is "_____" Greek.

Alexander wanted to "_____" all lands within the borders of his empire. This would fuse the Greek and _____ cultures. The new Greek dialect "_____" became the _____ language of the Mediterranean world.

The Greek language (is/is not) flexible.

2. The two pronunciations of the New Testament Greek are (1) the _____ pronunciation from the 16th century Dutch scholar Desiderius _____ and (2) the _____ Greek pronunciation.

The first pronunciation mentioned above (has/does not have) flaws. This pronunciation emphasizes the phonetic value of vowels and _____, which are not spoken in the _____ Greek. It is safe to assert that of the two pronunciation systems mentioned above, the _____ Greek is closer to the "Koine" period.

3. The Greek Alphabet. The Greek alphabet consists of _____ letters. After reading the information in Item 5, memorize the alphabet and practice writing it in the spaces by each letter. **Emphasize the lower case!**

alpha	A	α
beta	B	β
gamma	Γ	γ
delta	Δ	δ
epsilon	E	ε
zeta	Z	ζ
eta	H	η
theta	Θ	θ

yota	I	ι
kappa	K	κ
lambda	Λ	λ
mu	M	μ
nu	N	ν
xi	Ξ	ξ
omicron	O	ο
pi	Π	π
rho	P	ϱ
sigma	Σ	σ, ς
tau	T	τ
upsilon	Y	υ
phi	Φ	φ
khi	X	χ
psi	Ψ	ψ
omega	Ω	ω

4. Vowels and Diphthongs. There are _____vowels: ___, ___, ___, ___, ___, ___, and ___. There are _____ consonants.

Of the vowels:

___ and ___ are always long,

___ and ___ are always short,

___, ___ and ___ are sometimes long or _____ and are called

_____.

When two (vowels/consonants) are fused, this forms a _____. A diphthong has _____ vowels. The ___ or the ___ are added to vowels to form a diphthong.

The iota (ι) subscript—written below the line—may be added to these vowels: ___, ___, and ___. The pronunciation (is not/is) changed.

When **αι** or **οι** is at the end of a word, it is (short/long).

Two dots (ϊ) above the second vowel indicate that the combination of vowels is not a _____. The sign is called "_____."

5. Learn to pronounce the Greek alphabet.

6. The phonetic value of diphthongs in modern Greek is:

αι) like **ε** as in _____.

ει) like **η** as in _____.

οι) like **η** as in _____.

υι) like **η** as in _____.

ου) like **oo** as in _____.

Modern Greek pronunciation treats diphthongs as a _____ vowel without changing the sound:

αυ, ευ, ηυ, are pronounced as **"af," "ef," "eef"** if followed by the consonants ___, ___, ___, ___, ___, ___, ___, ___, ___; or as, **"av," "ev," "eev"** if followed by a _____; or the consonants ___, ___, ___, ___, ___, ___, ___, ___.

ωϋ (is not/is) a diphthong. Pronounce Μωϋσῆς.

7. Consonants. These nine are classified as stops:

	Labials	Dentals	Gutturals
Hard	_____	_____	_____
Soft	_____	_____	_____
Aspirate	_____	_____	_____

Two of the consonants, ____ and ____ are nasals. Two others, ____ and ____ are liquids.

The "ng" sound is produced when _____ or _____ (as in anger) follows the consonant γ, but when followed by _____ the sound is "_____," as in ma<u>nh</u>ood.

8. Syllables. How many syllables does a word have?

_____.

The last three syllables of a word are called the _____, _____ and _____. Which is the last syllable? _____ Accents are placed on the last (three/four) syllables. A syllable is considered long, if it has a (long/short) vowel or _____.

Syllables are formed in the following manner:

(i) The consonant _____ the vowel: Divide καλός _____.

(ii) <u>Two</u> <u>or</u> <u>more</u> consonants may precede the vowel. Divide χριστός: _____ and λαμβάνω: _____.

(iii) A syllable (cannot/can) begin with more than one of the same consonant.

Divide θάλασσα _____. Note the double (σ).

9. Punctuation.

(i) The full-stop period [.] and comma (,) are the (same/different) as in English.

(ii) Put a Greek semicolon after this word: κυρίου __.

(iii) Put a Greek question mark after this word: κυρίου __.

Lesson 2

Breathings ● *Accents* ● *Elision*

1. Breathings. All words beginning with a vowel or _____ have a breathing mark over the single vowel or over the (first/second) vowel of the _____.
What are the names of the two breathing marks? _____ and _____.

(ʼ) is _____ ; breath held back.
(ʽ) is _____ ; breath goes out: "h" sound–ha, he, etc. (soft).

Memorize these three rules, and apply correct breathing mark:

(i) The vowel **υ** at the beginning of the word always takes the (rough/smooth) breathing. Put the proper breathing on **υιος**. (Note that the breathing mark is over the second vowel.)

(ii) The definite article (the) when it consists of a vowel or _____ takes the rough breathing. Put the proper breathing on **οι**.

(iii) If **ϱ** begins a word, it takes the (rough/smooth) breathing.

2. Accents. As a rule, _____ words have an accent. The two exceptions are words that have ___ accent and words that have ____ accents. The three accents are:

(i) _____
(ii) _____
(iii) _____

3. The accent can only be placed on one of the last _____ syllables. The second vowel of the _____ is accented. The breathing mark is placed (before/after) the acute or _____ accent and (above/beneath) the circumflex. Accent with a smooth breathing on the first syllable: ανθϱωπος and οινος.

4. Correct to reflect the general rules of accent:

(i) The accent cannot be placed on the antepenult if the ultima is (short/long).

(ii) The noun is inflected and has _____ cases. The pattern is set by the _____ case. If permissible, the accent is retained on the same syllable as in the _____. Accent the following: ἀποστολος, ἀποστολου, ἀποστολον.

(iii) The verb rule of accent: The accent is placed as far from the _____ as possible, in accordance with rule (i). Accent λαμβανω (long ultima) and ἐλαμβανον (short ultima).

5

5. Basic rules are:

(i) The _____ may be placed on any of the last three syllables.
The _____ may be placed on either of the last two.
The _____ may be placed only on the ultima (last).

(ii) The circumflex is never on a (short/long) syllable.

(iii) If a long penult is accented, it must receive the acute if the ultima is _____, and a circumflex if the ultima is _____.

(iv) Two conditions mark the use of the grave accent in place of the acute accent: it is used only on the (penult, ultima) when there (is, is not,) a punctuation mark immediatley following.

6. Elision. An _____ is used to show that a letter has been dropped. This is done on certain words when an accented ultima ends in a vowel and precedes a word beginning with a _____. παρ᾽ αὐτοῦ stands for _____ αὐτοῦ.

GENERAL RULES OF ACCENT

ANTEPENULT	PENULT	ULTIMA	ACCENT
/	/	/	Acute
	~	~	Circumflex
		\	Grave

The circumflex (does not/does) stand on a short _____ or _____.

PENULT	ULTIMA	ACCENT
/ if accented	Long	Acute
Long ~if accented	Short	Circumflex
	Long / or ~	Acute or Circumflex
	if word follows without punctuation	Acute changes to Grave

VERB ACCENT

ANTEPENULT	PENULT	ULTIMA
/		Short
	/	Long

Lesson 3

Parts of Speech ● *Parsing*
The Verb: Present Active Indicative
The Conjunction: καί

1. Parts of Speech. Give examples of the parts of speech: the _____, the _____, the _____, the _____, the _____, and the _____.

2. Parsing. In parsing, a word is grammatically (i) _____ with one of these groups and (ii) its _____ _____ (parts) are given.

3. The Verb. The verb has a _____ role in a sentence. A complete sentence always has a _____.

4. Transitive and Intransitive Verbs. A verb may express an action or a _____ of _____. A transitive verb shows _____ on something other than the subject. An intransitive verb expresses no _____ _____ (e.g. I stand).

5. The direct object receives the action of the _____. The direct object may have an _____ object indicating _____ or _____ _____ the action is performed.

6. Distinctive Features of the Verb. Give the five features:

(i) _____. This expresses a time element.

(a) _____, _____, or _____;
(b) duration of the _____;
(c) the relation to the _____ some other action takes place;
(d) whether or not the action is viewed as _____ at the time of writing.

(ii) _____. The two _____ in English are _____ and _____ Greek has a middle _____, also.

(iii) _____. The six _____ are:

_____   _____

_____   _____

_____   _____ (rarely used)

9

(iv) _____. Identifies the one performing or being affected by the action. One of three: _____, _____ or a _____ party is designated as performing the action.

(v) _____. _____ (one person) or _____ (more than one person).

7. Stem and Ending. The _____ remains basically unchanged. The _____ varies according to voice, mood, etc. In English it is the personal pronoun which expresses the subject, in Greek it is the _____ which expresses it, though the personal pronoun may be used for _____.

8. To find the stem of a verb in this lesson, eliminate the _____ from the first person singular.

9. The endings of the present indicative active are:

	Singular	**Plural**
1st person	-_____ I	-_____ we
2nd person	-_____ thou (you)	-_____ you
3rd person	-_____ he, she, it	-_____ they

The **ν** in the third person plural is called a "_____ ν," and may or may not be used.

10. There is no distinction in Greek from "I write" and "___ ___ _____."

11. It is advisable to use _____ . . . _____ for the second person singular.

12. To form a question in Greek, the _____ _____ is added at the end of the sentence (;).

13. The Conjunction. The conjunction links _____ or more words in a sentence or _____ or more sentences. _____ (and) is the most common.

(Parse the verbs on the next page.)

PARSING EXERCISES

When parsing a verb, the tense, voice, mood, person, number and the root word from which it comes should be given. Example: λύομεν is present, active, indicative, first person plural from λύω. You may abbreviate e.g. Pres., Act., Ind., 1, Pl.

Parse the following verbs. (Personal endings are underscored.)

From	Parse	Tense	Voice	Mood	Person	Sing./Pl.
λύω	λύει	Pres.	Act.	Ind.	3	Sing.
	βλέπομεν					
	γράφεις					
	διδάσκει					
	λαμβάνετε					
	λύετε					
	ἔχεις					
	γράφουσι					
	λαμβάνουσι					
	γινώσκομεν					
	λύομεν					
	λέγει					
	βλέπει					
	διδάσκω					
	γινώσκω					

Did you notice that by adding the ω to the verb stem that you always know the root word from which the verb to be parsed came from? REMEMBER THIS! Very soon the tense, voice and mood will change.

Lesson 4

The Noun
Nouns of the Second Declension
The Indefinite Article

1. Distinctive Features of the Noun.

(i) _____: There are _____ cases.

    (a) _____. The noun serving as the _____ of the verb.

    (b) _____. A noun expressing "_____."

    (c) _____. The chief role of the noun, indicating the _____ object.

    (d) _____. The noun indicates the _____ object of the verb. A small number of verbs may have the direct object in the _____ or _____.

    (e) _____. The noun indicating _____ _____.

(ii) _____:List the three:_____, _____, _____.

(iii) _____: _____ and _____.

(iv) There are three _____. As a rule each has (different/the same) endings.

2. Stem and Endings.

The _____ remains basically unchanged in all cases and both numbers. The _____ varies in the two numbers, and the cases but not necessarily in all of them.

3.

There is no set order of words in the Greek sentence. The ending of a word determines the part of speech for any noun.

Nominative case	ἀπόστολος	the subject
Verb	διδάσκει	the verb
Accusative case	δοῦλον	the direct object

Using the words above, form three sentences that are in correct word order:

    (a) _____

    (b) _____

    (c) _____

The Greek language is (flexible/rigid). Find the verb first and proceed to the noun (or an _____, _____, or participle) in the _____ case; it will be the _____ of the verb. Then search for a noun in the accusative (object) or dative (indirect object), etc.

4. Nouns of the Second Declension. This is the (easiest/hardest) declension and it covers (many/few) of the NT words.

5. Endings. Masculine and feminine nouns have the _____ endings. What determines the gender? _____ _____. Fill in the blanks for the endings

	Masculine and Feminine		Neuter	
	Singular	**Plural**	**Singular**	**Plural**
Nom.	-_____	-_____	-_____	-_____
Gen.	-_____	-_____	-_____	-_____
Dat.	-_____	-_____	-_____	-_____
Acc.	-_____	-_____	-_____	-_____
Voc.	-_____	-_____	-_____	-_____

Complete the following (apostle, way, child) with accents:

	Masculine	**Feminine**	**Neuter**
		Singular	
Nom.	ἀπόστολ____	ὁδ____	τέκν____
Gen.	ἀποστολ____	ὁδ____	τεκν____
Dat.	ἀποστολ____	ὁδ____	τεκν____
Acc.	ἀποστολ____	ὁδ____	τεκν____
Voc.	ἀποστολ____	ὁδ____	τεκν____
		Plural	
Nom.	ἀποστολ____	ὁδ____	τεκν____
Gen.	ἀποστολ____	ὁδ____	τεκν____
Dat.	ἀποστολ____	ὁδ____	τεκν____
Acc.	ἀποστολ____	ὁδ____	τεκν____
Voc.	ἀποστολ____	ὁδ____	τεκν____

6. If the ultima in the genitive and dative is accented, it is the _____.

7. The Indefinite Article (a/an). No _____ article exists in Greek.

8. Neuter Plural Subject. Neuter Plural nouns are frequently considered as collective nouns and therefore take a _____ verb.

οἱ ἄνθρωποι	διδάσκουσιν	τοὺς νόμους	τοῖς ἀνθρώποις
The men (Subject)	teach (Verb)	the laws (Direct Object)	to the men (Indirect Object)

οἱ ἄνθρωποι	Subject – In the <u>Nominative Case</u>, Masculine, Plural
διδάσκουσιν	Action Verb – Pres. Act. Ind., Third Person, Plural, (from _____).
τοὺς νόμους	Direct Object – In the <u>Accusative Case</u>, Masculine, Plural
τοῖς ἀνθρώποις	Indirect Object – In the <u>Dative Case</u>, Masculine, Plural

The correct English wording is: "The men teach the laws (to) the men."

You will notice that the endings of nouns, pronouns, and adjectives will give identification for case, gender, and number. If a definite article is used, it will also agree in case, gender, and number.

Declining Exercises

Nouns have case, gender, and number and are indentified by being declined. Verbs are parsed, nouns are declined, however the term parse or parsing is often applied to both. The stem of the noun defines it and the endings give the case, gender and number.

Example: ἄνθρωπος – The stem is ἄνθρωπ- and the ending is -ος, which is nominative, masculine, and singular. You may abbreviate, e.g.; Nom., Masc., Sing.

Decline (identify) the following nouns:

From	Noun	Case	Gender	Sing./Pl.
ἄνθρωπος	ἄνθρωπ<u>ον</u>	Acc.	Masc.	Sing.
	ἀπόστολ<u>οι</u>			
	δούλ<u>ους</u>			
	ἀδελφ<u>οί</u>			
	ἱερ<u>ά</u>			
	ἀποστόλ<u>ους</u>			
	ἀποστόλ<u>ῳ</u>			
	νόμ<u>ον</u>*			
	δῶρ<u>α</u>			
	θάνατ<u>ον</u>*			
	δούλ<u>ου</u>			
	υἱ<u>οί</u>*			
	ἀνθρώπ<u>ου</u>			
	ἀποστόλ<u>ων</u>			
	λόγ<u>ον</u>			

*See Greek–English vocabulary on pages 271–298 to look up these words (p. 288 for νόμ<u>ον</u>, ου, ὁ).

Note: By adding **ος** or **ον** to the stem of the word, you have the root word from which the noun came. There will be a change in this later in the feminine gender.

Lesson 5

The Noun
Nouns of the First Declension
The Definite Article

1. Nouns of the First Declension. As to gender, the majority of these nouns are _____, but some _____ nouns are included. The endings in both genders are (the same/different) in the plural.

2. Feminine Nouns. The first groups end (case endings) in _____, if the stem ends in vowel or ϱ the case ending repeats the _____ in all the singulars. The second group case endings are determined by the end of the stem. If the stem end in λ, ξ, σ, or φ, the α will lengthen to _____ in the genitive and dative singular. The third group case endings are determined by any other consonants. The α lengthens to _____ in all singular forms.

3. Give the feminine endings for this declension:

	First Group	Second Group Singular	Third Group	All Groups Plural
Nom.	_____	_____	_____	_____
Gen.	_____	_____	_____	_____
Dat.	_____	_____	_____	_____
Acc.	_____	_____	_____	_____
Voc.	_____	_____	_____	_____

Complete the examples of the three sets of endings (church, tongue, prayer) with correct accents:

Singular

N.	ἐκκλησί____	γλῶσσ____	προσευχ____
G.	ἐκκλησι____	γλωσσ____	προσευχ____
D.	ἐκκλησι____	γλωσσ____	προσευχ____
A.	ἐκκλησι____	γλωσσ____	προσευχ____
V.	ἐκκλησι____	γλωσσ____	προσευχ____

Plural

N.	ἐκκλησι____	γλωσσ____	προσευχ____
G.	ἐκκλησι____	γλωσσ____	προσευχ____
D.	ἐκκλησι____	γλωσσ____	προσευχ____
A.	ἐκκλησι____	γλωσσ____	προσευχ____
V.	ἐκκλησι____	γλωσσ____	προσευχ____

5. Masculine Nouns. Give the most used masculine endings in the first declension:

	Singular	**Plural**
N.	-____	-____
G.	-____	-____
D	-____	-____
A.	-____	-____
V.	-____	-____

6. Complete the following:

	Singular	**Plural**
N.	τελών____	τελῶν____
G.	τελών____	τελων____
D.	τελών____	τελών____
A.	τελών____	τελών____
V.	τελῶν____	τελῶν____

7. Proper nouns may end in _____ in the nominative singular.

8. Rules of Accent. The nouns of the first declension, both masculine and feminine, seem to present an irregularity in the rule which governs the accent, in that the _____ plural moves the _____ accent to the ultima. Thus, βασιλεία and βασιλειῶν are not accented according to the rule of accent for nouns as we have learned them so far.

9. If the ultima is accented, the genitive and dative will have the _____ on both the singular and plural.

10. The Definite Article. "The" has basically the same meaning in _____ as in English. _____ nouns (e.g. truth) normally are preceded by the article.

11. The Greek article has _____ genders and (must/must not) agree with the word it accompanies.

12. The masculine and neuter articles are similar to the endings of the masculine and neuter _____ of the _____ declension. The feminine article is declined like the -___ ending group of the _____ declension.

NOTICE:

(i) the dropping of the -ς in the _____ singular.

(ii) the neuter article dropping the final ν in the nominative and _____ singular.

(iii) the consonant ___ prefixed to the noun endings of the 1st and 2nd declensions, with the exception of the nominative masculine and feminine in both numbers.

13. The masculine and feminine article in the nominative of both numbers takes the _____ breathing.

14. Following the pattern of the noun of the first and second declensions, the article in all three genders takes the circumflex in the _____ and _____ in both numbers.

15. The article has no vocative. In its place ____ is used as an exclamation.

16. Decline the article: (including the breathing marks and accents.)

	Singular			Plural		
	Mas.	Fem.	Neu.	Mas.	Fem.	Neu.
N.	____	____	____	____	____	____
G.	____	____	____	____	____	____
D.	____	____	____	____	____	____
A.	____	____	____	____	____	____

17. The article is the same gender as the noun it accompanies whether or not the ending differs. Do not be confused by the noun ending. Fill in the correct article: ____ προφῆται and ____ ὁδοί.

Lesson 6

The Negative:

οὐ . . . μή • μέν . . . δέ • οὐδέ

καί . . . καί

1. The Negative. Negation is expressed by _____, in the indicative and ___ is used for all other moods. The negative is placed (in front/ behind) the word it affects. When a vowel or diphthong follows, **οὐ** becomes _____, and if the following vowel has a rough breathing, it changes to_____.

2. If **οὐ** stands alone and is accented (**οὔ**), it means "_____."

3. Emphasis is expressed by _____, or by _____ and _____.

4. μέν...δέ. These introduce a _____, or may be translated as the expression "_____ _____ _____ _____ . . . _____ _____ _____ _____." In many instances it is advisable to leave **μέν** _____, and proceed to translate **δέ** as_____ or ____. Whenever these two words are preceded by the article, usually in the plural and not followed by nouns, they may mean "_____ . . . _____."

5. If **δέ** is preceded by the _____, it is translated "and (but) (___/_____)." ὁ δὲ λέγει means "_____ (_____) _____ _____."

6. οὐδέ is a combination of _____ and _____. οὐδὲ . . . οὐδὲ means "_____ . . . _____."

7. καί . . . καί means "_____ . . . _____."

8. καί may also mean "_____," or "_____." Translate: καὶ οἱ δοῦλοι γράφουσι. "_____ the slaves are writing," or "the slaves _____ are waiting."

Lesson 7

The Adjective:
Adjectives of the First and Second Declensions

1. The Adjective. The adjective supplies information about certain properties or _____ of a person or _____.

2. The adjective is declined and must agree in _____, _____, and _____ with the noun it qualifies.

3. Attributive and Predicative Adjective.

The faithful disciple – is the _____ use of the adjective

This disciple is faithful – is the _____ use of the adjective

4. The auxiliary verb "_____" may or may not be used in Greek.

   (i) The attributive adjective (follows/precedes) the article.

   (ii) The predicative adjective (never/always) follows the article.

5. Identify the following constructions (attributive or predicative).

ὁ ἀγαθὸς ἀπόστολος   _____.

ἀγαθὸς ὁ ἀπόστολος   _____.

ὁ ἀπόστολος ὁ ἀγαθός   _____.

ὁ ἀπόστολος ἀγαθός   _____.

Note the position of the article.

6. Context determines translation of the adjective when it (does not have/has) the article. ἀπόστολος ἀγαθὸς may mean "___ _____ _____," or "___ _____ ___ _____."

7. Adjective used as a noun. οἱ ἀγαθοί may mean "___ _____ _____."

8. Adjectives of the First and Second Declensions. Adjectives, like nouns, belong to one of the _____ declensions.

9. Adjectives whose stems end in a vowel or ϱ decline like feminine lst declension nouns of the ___ class. Those with stems ending in a consonant other than ϱ decline like the first declension nouns of the ___ class. Give the feminine form of the nominative adjective and the stem in the feminine gender for δίκαιος _____, and ἀγαθός, ἀγαθ_____.

10. Compound adjectives are formed by:

    (i) Prefixing **(a)** a _____: περίλυπος, **ον**; **(b)** the privative **α** or **αν**, and it equals the English "_____": ἄπιστος, **ον**; **(c)** an _____ like **ευ**; εὐάρεστος, **ον**.

    (ii) Suffixing to a NT noun the endings -ιος and -ιμος; αἰών_____, ὠφέλ_____.

11. The feminine adjective in the genitive plural (always/does not always) accent the ultima: Accent the following: τῶν δικαιων βασιλειῶν.

Lesson 8

The Verb: Imperfect Active Indicative
The Conjunction ὅτι

1. Imperfect Indicative Active. This is a _____ tense, not present.

2. The past tenses denote _____ action, or _____ for all in the past.

3. The imperfect is used for a _____ or _____ action in the past. It is called "(linear/punctiliar)" and represented by a line (––––––>). Other past action is represented by a dot (•) and is called "(linear/punctiliar)."

4. "Tendential Imperfect" represents _____ action, which may not actually be performed.

5. The imperfect is found only in the _____ mood.

6. Imperfect endings are added to the _____. Give the endings.

To form the imperfect the **ω** is dropped from the present active indicative, first person singular to find the stem of the **ω**-verbs.

Singular		**Plural**	
-_____	I	-_____	we
-_____	thou	-_____	you
-_____	he, she, it	-_____	they

7. Augment. Endings are added (before/after) the stem, while the augment is added (before/after) the stem in the imperfect, the aorist and the pluperfect.

(i) In verbs beginning with a consonant, the augment _____ is added and is pronounced separately. This is a "_____" augment. Thus, the imperfect of γράφω is ἔγραφον.

(ii) When verbs begin with a vowel, the vowel is (lengthened/shortened) forming a "<u>temporal</u>" augment. Give the changes.

$$\alpha \quad = \quad \underline{\hspace{2em}}$$
$$\varepsilon \quad = \quad \underline{\hspace{2em}} \quad (\text{Exception: } ἔχω = \underline{\hspace{3em}}).$$
$$o \quad = \quad \underline{\hspace{2em}}$$

(iii) Verbs beginning with a diphthong undergo a change: Give the changes.

αι = _____

ει = _____

οι = _____

αυ= _____

ευ = _____ or may remain unchanged.

If the initial vowel in the stem has the rough breathing it (is/is not) retained.

In order to tell the stem of a verb, consult an analytical lexicon. Learn to recognize that the verb has an augment (syllabic or temporal) and then determine its origin (stem): ἤκουον may be from _____ or _____.

8. Rule of the Accent. When the ultima is short the accent may go back to the _____. Place the accent: ἀκούω = long ultima–penult accented. ἤκουον = short ultima–antepenult accented.

9. ὅτι. This conjunction is used to render one of the following services:

(i) as "that" to denote _____ or _____ quotations. It may come first in the clause, thus it is not _____.

(ii) as "because" to link _____ sentence (clauses) with the main one.

10. Ἰησοῦς. Complete the declension:

Notice that, without the articles, there is no way to distinguish the genitive form from the dative form, and that both resemble the vocative form.

N.	ὁ	Ἰησ_____
G.	τοῦ	Ἰησ_____
D.	τῷ	Ἰησ_____
A.	τὸν	Ἰησ_____
V.		Ἰησ_____

Lesson 9

The Preposition:
Prepositions with One and Two Cases

1. The Preposition. A preposition is a word which, when placed before a noun or pronoun, expresses the _____ which exists between the word being modified and its object.

2. The Greek preposition may have more than one meaning. The _____ (genitive, dative, accusative) determines the meaning. When memorizing prepositions, it is helpful to say: ἀντί with the genitive ("instead of") etc.

3. List with each preposition the case in which it is used and the meaning with that case.

Prepositions	Case	Meaning
ἀνά	_____	_____
ἀντί	_____	_____
ἀπό	_____	_____
ἐκ	_____	_____
ἐν	_____	_____
εἰς	_____	_____
πρό	_____	_____
σύν	_____	_____

4. List the prepositions that are used with two cases and their meanings in each case.

Prepositions	Case	Meaning
διά	_____	_____
	_____	_____
κατά	_____	_____
	_____	_____
μετά	_____	_____
	_____	_____
περί	_____	_____
	_____	_____
πρός	_____	_____

ὑπέρ   _____   _____

ὑπό   _____   _____

5. Elision. Elision usually occurs when a preposition ending with a _____ is followed by a word that begins with a _____. περί and πρό (are not/are) affected by this rule. Give the changes that take place in the vowel of the following word by listing the rough breathings, and the smooth.

	Rough	**Smooth**
ἀπό becomes	ἀφ'	ἀπ'
ἐπί	_____	_____
ἀντί	_____	_____
κατά	_____	_____
μετά	_____	_____

These are also found in the Greek NT.

ἀνά	ἀν	ἀν'
διά	δι'	δι'
παρά	παρ'	παρ'

Lesson 10

The Preposition: Prepositions with Three Cases
The Verb: Present Indicative of the Verb εἰμί
Proclitics and Enclitics
The English Preparatory "There"

1. Prepositions: How many prepositions have three cases? _____ Give them and their meanings in all three cases.

Preposition		Meaning According to Case.
_____	Gen.	_____
_____	Dat.	_____
_____	Acc.	_____
_____	Gen.	_____
_____	Dat.	_____
_____	Acc.	_____

2. Present Indicative of the Verb εἰμί **— "to be."**

Complete the conjugation:

_____	I am	_____	we are
_____	thou art	_____	you are
_____	he, she, it is	_____	they are

3. εἰμί does not take an object; instead a _____ of the subject is used to complete its meaning: ὁ μαθητὴς ἀγαθός is translated "The disciple (<u>is</u>) good." Important! Do not use the accusative case with εἰμί: it takes the _____ case.

4. The verb εἰμί and other verbs do not take the accusative case (direct object). The verb _____: *I become*, and others also take a predicate <u>nominative</u>.

5. When two nouns are linked as subject and predicate nominative with the verb εἰμί and one has the article and the other does not, which one is the subject, regardless of word order? Answer: The one with _____ _____.

6. Proclitics and Enclitics. Proclitics and enclitics are two groups of words that form exceptions to the rule of _____.

7. Proclitics. These words under normal conditions have **no accent of their own.** These are the principal proclitics:

29

(i) The masculine article: ___, ___, and feminine article, ___, ___ in the nominative of both singular and plural numbers.

(ii) The prepositions _____, _____, _____.

(iii) The negative _____.

(iv) The words _____ (if) and _____ (as).

8. Enclitics. The enclitics are words that go so closely with the words that _____ them, they lose their accent or it transfers to the _____ word. Study these enclitics. The enclitics are:

(i) The verbs _____ and _____ in the present indicative, with the exception of the second person singular εἶ.

(ii) μου, μοι, με, σου, σοι, σε are (unemphatic/emphatic) – no accent.

(iii) The indefinite pronoun _____.

(iv) The conjunction _____ and the adverbs _____, _____, _____, and

_____.

9. Rules Which Govern. An enclitic should be read as a _____ of the preceding word for reasons of euphony. Place the proper accents on examples.

(i) One syllable enclitics _____ their accent or _____ it to the preceding word: ὁ θεος μου, "_____."

(ii) A two-syllable enclitic retains its accent only when the preceding word has an accent on the _____. ἡ θυρα ἐστιν, "_____."

(iii) If the preceding word would have a grave, it changes to an _____: e.g. "ὁδος τις, _____ _____."

(iv) If the word preceding an enclitic has a circumflex on the penult or an acute on the _____, it receives the accent of the enclitic as a second accent in the form of (a/an) acute on the ultima. ὁ οικος μου; διδασκαλοι ἐσμεν.

(v) If the enclitic is preceded by a _____, it receives the accent of the enclitic in the form of an _____ (εκ τινος).

(vi) An acute is placed on the (first/second) enclitic when one follows the other (δοῦλοί μου εἰσιν).

10. The 3rd person singular of the verb _____ (does/does not) lose its accent, but has it on the _____ when:

(i) it means "_____."

(ii) it is after _____ and some other words.

11. The Preparatory "There." The preparatory "there" is not used in the (English/Greek) language.

Lesson 11

1. The Compound Verbs. _____ may be prefixed to verbs to form a compound verb.

2. The effects of attaching prepositions to verbs:

(i) The original meaning of the verb may be _____. γινώσκω means I know; ἐπιγινώσκω means _____.

(ii) It ____ _____ the meaning of the original verb. ἄγω means I lead; ἀπάγω: ___ _____ _____. ἐγκαταλείπω is from the original verb _____. _____ prepositions precede λείπω.

(iii) An entirely _____ meaning may be produced. γινώσκω: ___ _____; ἀναγινώσκω: ___ _____.

(iv) It may produce no discernible _____ in meaning. Thus λαμβάνω and παραλαμβάνω both mean essentially, ____ _____.

3. Often the attached preposition (is/is not) repeated in the sentence.

4. Elision takes place when the preposition ends with a vowel and the verb begins with a vowel. The prepositions _____ and _____ are excluded from this rule. ἐκ becomes _____ when the original verb begins with a vowel and before the _____ of the imperfect and aorist tenses.

5. Though not always in the NT, the "**ν**" of the prepositions _____ and _____:

(i) Turns to **μ** before ____, ____, ____ (labials).
(ii) Turns to **γ** before ____, ____, ____ (gutturals).
(iii) Turns to **λ** before ____.
(iv) Is dropped before ____ and ____ (σύν only).

6. Present and Imperfect Indicative. Compound verbs are conjugated (differently/exactly) as the original verb. The augment comes (after/before) the preposition and is attached to the original verb (προσφέρω – προσέφερον). The accent <u>cannot</u> be placed on the _____ (συνάγω – συνῆγον).

31

Lesson
12

The Pronoun:
The Personal Pronoun

1. The Pronoun. Generally a pronoun is used in the place of a _____.

2. The word for which a pronoun is used is called the "_____." "We love God (antecedent) and worship <u>Him</u> (pronoun)." List the eight kinds of pronouns:

_____ _____ _____

_____ _____ _____

_____ _____

3. The Personal Pronoun. _____ persons are found in the personal pronoun, and in the third person there are _____ genders as in English (I, thou, he [masculine], she [feminine], it [neuter]).

4. The personal pronoun is declined like a _____ or _____. It agrees with its antecedent in _____ and number, but not necessarily in _____. ἐπιστολή is a feminine noun, so the Greek pronoun that modifies it will be _____ (feminine), not _____ (neuter).

5. The 1st and 2nd person endings are similiar in the singular and _____ cases in the plural. The third person has _____ declension endings in the masculine and the neuter, with the neuter dropping the **ν** in the _____ and _____ singular. The feminine is formed in the _____ declension of the _____ group endings.

6. The personal pronoun is used in Greek to place _____ on the subject. διδάσκω: _____, but ἐγώ διδάσκω: I _____ teach. Emphasis is used to show explicit _____ or _____ between the subjects of two verbs. Translate: ἐγώ εἰμί δοῦλος, σύ δὲ εἶ ὁ κύριος, I am a _____ but _____ art _____ _____.

7. Complete the declension of the personal pronoun with breathing and accent marks:

First Person			**Second Person**	
			Singular	
N.ἐγ___		I	σύ	thou
G.____ or ____		of me	____	of thee
D.____ or ____		to/for me	____	to/for thee
A.____ or ____		me	____	thee

33

Plural

N.ἡμ___	we		ὑμ___	you	
G._____	of us		_____	of you	
D._____	to/for us		_____	to/for you	
A._____	us		_____	you	

Third Person

	Singular			Plural	
Masc.	**Fem.**	**Neut.**	**Masc.**	**Fem.**	**Neut.**
N.αὐτ___ he,	αὐτ___ she,	αὐτ___ it,	αὐτ___ they,	αὐτ___	αὐτ___
G.αὐτ___	αὐτ___	αὐτ___	αὐτ___	αὐτ___	αὐτ___
D.αὐτ___	αὐτ___	αὐτ___	αὐτ___	αὐτ___	αὐτ___
A.αὐτ___	αὐτ___	αὐτ___	αὐτ___	αὐτ___	αὐτ___

8. The accented forms in first person in the genitive, dative and accusative singular are _____; the unaccented form is an _____.

9. The unemphatic form in the genitive is used to express _____. τὸ βιβλίον μου: "_____ _____," ὁ διδάσκαλος ὑμῶν: "_____ _____."

10. Elision takes place when a preposition ending in ___ _____ is used before a pronoun (as in case of the noun) beginning with a vowel. The emphatic form is used in this 1st person singular. Thus παρά μου becomes _____ ἐμοῦ, _____ ἐμοί, _____ ἐμέ. πρός with the accusative may be followed by either the _____ or _____ form of the pronoun. Thus "to me" may be written either: πρὸς _____, or πρός _____.

11. The third person may be used together with a _____, and has one of two different meanings.

(i) If the pronoun follows the article (the _____ position), it means "___ _____." Μέν, δέ, and γάρ may come between the article and pronoun. Thus, τὸ δὲ αὐτὸ πνεῦμα: "but the _____ Spirit."

(ii) When the pronoun does not follow the article (the _____ position), it is used for purposes of _____–thus, αὐτὸς ὁ θεὸς τῆς εἰρήνης: "The God ___ ____ _____."

12. Emphasis may be expressed or implied by using two pronouns together. ἐγὼ αὐτὸς γράφω: "I _____ write." αὐτοὶ οἴδατε: "you _____ know." αὐτοὶ is used to emphasize all plural nouns or pronouns: "we ourselves, you yourselves, they themselves."

Lesson 13

The Pronoun: The Demonstrative Pronouns
The Adjective: Comparison of Adjectives

1. The Demonstrative Pronouns. The Demonstrative Pronouns point out and _____ certain objects in distinction from others.

2. The two principal demonstrative pronouns in the NT Greek are: (this) _____(m.), _____(f.), _____(n.) and (that) _____, _____, _____.

3. ὅδε, ἥδε, τόδε is a _____ demonstrative pronoun and used several times in the third plural with the meaning of "_____ _____."

4. The demonstrative pronouns:

(i) Are always in the _____ position when used with a noun, and agree with the noun they qualify in _____, _____, and _____. The article is (always/never) used with the noun. Thus, οὗτος _____ ἀπόστολος, or _____ ἀπόστολος οὗτος; ἐκεῖνος _____ δοῦλος, or _____ δοῦλος ἐκεῖνος.

(ii) (Can/cannot) stand alone. Translate οὗτος πιστεύει: _____ _____ _____.

5. Complete the declensions with accents and breathing:

	Singular			**Plural**		
	M.	**F.**	**N.**	**M.**	**F.**	**N.**
N.	οὗτ____	αυτ____	τουτ____	ουτ____	αυτ____	ταυτ____
G.	τουτ____	ταυτ____	τουτ____	τουτ____	τουτ____	τουτ____
D.	τουτ____	ταυτ____	τουτ____	τουτ____	ταυτ____	τουτ____
A.	τουτ____	ταυτ____	τουτ____	τουτ____	ταυτ____	ταυτ____
N.	ἐκειν____	ἐκειν____	ἐκειν____	ἐκειν____	ἐκειν____	ἐκειν____
G.	ἐκειν____	ἐκειν____	ἐκειν____	ἐκειν____	ἐκειν____	ἐκειν____
D.	ἐκειν____	ἐκειν____	ἐκειν____	ἐκειν____	ἐκειν____	ἐκειν____
A.	ἐκειν____	ἐκειν____	ἐκειν____	ἐκειν____	ἐκειν____	ἐκειν____

6. Specific Features of the Demonstrative Pronouns.

(i) Both demonstrative pronouns have the regular endings of the first-second declension in all three genders, with the exception that the _____ drops the final **ν** in the nominative and the accusative _____.

(ii) The interchange of **αυ** and **ου** in the stem of οὗτος, αὕτη and τοῦτο is subject to the rule that **ου** is in the stem when there is an ___, or ___ in the ending; otherwise the stem has **αυ**.

(iii) The demonstrative pronoun has no _____ case.

(iv) The accents and breathings are different between the **demonstrative** pronoun (feminine) αὕτη, αὗται and the _____ pronoun αὐτή, αὐταί.

7. Comparison of the Adjectives. The adjective can be used in the absolute sense: "a good man," or it can indicate a comparison of the _____ it qualifies: i.e., "a better man," or "the best man." The three degrees in the adjective are: _____, _____, and _____.

8. Remembering that adjectives have all three genders, give the comparative endings for the three: -_____, -_____, -_____ and the superlative endings for the adjectives of the first and second declensions: -_____, -_____, and -_____.

9. The **o** at the beginning of these endings changes into ___, if the last vowel in the stem of the adjective is short. A difficulty occurs if the last vowel in the stem is one of the three "dichrons," ___, ___, ___, that can be either long or short. The problem can be reduced by these 2 rules.

(i) The **ι** is short in adjectives ending in -___, ___, ___, and ___.

(ii) All three "_____" are long if they are immediately followed by two or more consonants in a row.

10. A small number of commonly used adjectives change their form in the _____, or _____ degrees; or both, in an _____ way.

11. The irregular superlative of μικρός (smaller) is _____ (smallest, least).

12. The superlative degree is (always/never/rarely) used in the NT. The comparative is often used in the sense of the _____.

13. A comparison can be made either by putting the noun or pronoun with which the first one is compared in the _____ case, or having the particle ___ than follow the adjective and putting the second noun or pronoun in the same case as the first. Thus: σοφώτερος τοῦ ἀδελφοῦ αὐτοῦ, or σοφώτερος ἢ ὁ ἀδελφὸς αὐτοῦ.

Lesson 14

The Verb: Middle and Passive Voice:
Present and Imperfect Indicative
Deponent Verbs
Imperfect Indicative of the Verb εἰμί

1. The Middle and Passive Voices. In all languages a statement can be made in two forms: _____ and _____. Active: "The apostle teaches the disciple." Passive: "The disciple is _____ _____ by the disciple."

2. There is also a _____ voice in Greek.

3. To turn an active sentence into a passive one, the object in the active sentence becomes the _____. The previous subject becomes the "agent" by which the _____ is performed. "By" is expressed by "ὑπό" followed by the noun or adjective in the _____ case—a noun or adjective. ὑπό + genitive is used with a passive verb.

4. A noun in the _____ case is used to express the instrument or _____ that is used to bring about the action described. This is "impersonal," and is called the "dative of _____." It is best-translated "by _____ ___." Since the _____ object is also in the _____ case, the context is to be used to determine whether the dative case is used as an instrument or an indirect object.

5. Present and Imperfect Indicative. In the imperfect and present, the endings are the (same/different) in both the middle and passive voices. Remember the imperfect has an _____. Context determines whether the middle or passive voice is used. Give the endings of the Present and Imperfect Indicative:

Present		Imperfect	
- _____	- _____	- _____	- _____
- _____	- _____	- _____	- _____
- _____	- _____	- _____	- _____

Complete the conjugation of: λύω

Present

Middle		Passive	
λύ_____	I loose for myself	I ____ _____ loosed	
λύ_____	Thou loosest for thyself	Thou ____ _____ loosed	
λύ_____	He looses for himself	He ___ _____ loosed	

λύ_____	We loose for ourselves	We ____ _____ loosed
λύ_____	You loose for yourselves	You ____ _____ loosed
λύ_____	They loose for themselves	They ____ _____ loosed

Imperfect

Middle		**Passive**	
__ λυ_____	I was loosing for myself	I ____ _____ loosed
__ λύ_____	Thou wast loosing for thyself	Thou ____ _____ loosed
__ λύ_____	He was loosing for himself	He ____ _____ loosed
__ λυ_____	We were loosing for ourselves	We ____ _____ loosed
__ λύ_____	You were loosing for yourselves	You ____ _____ loosed
__ λύ_____	They were loosing for themselves	They ____ _____ loosed

6. The imperfect (has/does not have) an augment. In verbs beginning with a consonant, an ____ is prefixed to the verb stem.

7. Deponent Verbs are formed in the _____ voice, but active in meaning. πορεύομαι: _____ (translate as an active)!

8. Some other verbs are in the active voice in certain tenses, but in the _____ voice in others:

9. A few deponent verbs form the _____ and the aorist in the passive voice. Such verbs are marked in the vocabularies as "Passive deponent."

10. A few verbs have an entirely different meaning in the middle compared to the the active voice. E.g. Active: ἄρχω – _____. Middle: ἄρχομαι – _____. Note the difference in meaning.

11. Imperfect of the Verb εἰμί. Conjugate the imperfect indicative:

_____ I was	_____ or (_____) we were
_____ (_____) thou wast	_____ you were
_____ he, she, it was	_____ they were

Lesson
15

1. Distinctive Features of the Future Active. The _____ is the distinctive consonant of this tense.

Conjugate the future indicative of λύω:

λύ-___-_____   λύ___-_____
λύ-___-_____   λύ___-_____
λύ-___-_____   λύ___-_____

2. If the stem ends:

(i) In a labial: **π, __, ___ + σ = ψ** (ps); thus, πέμπω = _____.
(ii) In a guttural: **κ, __, ___ + σ = ξ** (ks); thus, ἄγω = _____.
(iii) In a dental: **τ, __, ___ + σ = σ;** thus, πείθω = _____.

3. Present and Verbal Stems. The two stems of many verbs are the present stem and _____ _____ on which the _____ and _____ are formed, and the verbal stem (the original or basic stem) used to form the other tenses.

The three main groups are:

(i) The present stem, which ends in **σσ**, usually has verbal stem endings in ____. = φυλακ verbal stem. Give the future for φυλάσσω _____.

(ii) The present stem, which ends in **ζ**, usually has a verbal stem that ends in ____. Give the future for βαπτίζω _____.

Exception κράζω = _____.

(iii) The present stem, which ends in **ππ**, usually has verbal stem endings in ____. Give the future for κρύπτω: _____.

5. Verb stems which end with a nasal (___, or ___) or a liquid (___, or ___) consonant, form the future and aorist active, middle and passive in a special way and will be dealt with separately in Lesson 22.

6. Give the form of these that have irregular formations for the future.

Present	Future
ἁμαρτάνω	ἁμαρτ_____
δεικνύω	δεί_____
διδάσκω	διδά_____
εὑρίσκω	εὑρ_____
κλαίω	κλ_____
κράζω	κρά_____
φέρω	_____ (completely different).

7. The future of:
ἔχω is _____.
βλέπω is _____.
ὁράω is _____.

The verb λέγω forms its active future on the stem _____.

8. λύσω can mean "_____ _____ _____" or "_____ _____ ___ _____"—no distinction between continuous or non-continuous action.

Lesson 16

The Verb: Future Indicative Middle and Passive
Future of the Verb εἰμί
The Adjective: μέγας, πολύς

1. Distinctive Features of the Future Indicative Middle and Passive. The consonant ___ is used in the middle voice of the future tense.

2. _____ is used in the future passive voice.

3. Some verbs add the -___- between the stem and the sign of the future passive, _____; thus, ἀκούω becomes _____.

4. Complete the conjugation of the future middle and passive of λύω with accents:

Middle	**Passive**
λύ_____ I shall loose for myself	λυ_____ I shall be loosed
λύ_____	λυ_____
λύ_____	λυ_____
λύ_____	λυ_____
λύ_____	λυ_____
λύ_____	λυ_____

5. The same rules in Lesson **15 § 2** apply to the future middle formations. Thus, ἄγω becomes _____ (ἀκ-σο-μαι).

6. Adjustments are made to rules outlined in Lesson **15 § 3** in regards to the **θη** of the passive.

   (i) When the verbal stem ends in a labial (__, __, ___), it turns into a ___ before the θ. καλύπτω = καλυπ. Future: καλυ_____.

   (ii) When the verbal stem ends in a guttural (__, __, ___), it turns into _____ before the θ (κηρύσσω = κηρυκ); future: κηρυ_____.

   (iii) When the verbal stem ends in a dental (__, __, ___) before the θ, it turns into ___ before the θ.

Give the future passive for βαπτίζω: _____. Give the future passive for πείθω, _____. Give the future passive for σῴζω, _____. Give the future passive for ἐμπαίζω (I mock): ἐμπαι, _____.

41

7. Give the irregular formations of the future passive:

βάλλω	_____	εὑρίσκω	_____
βλέπω	_____	λαμβάνω	_____
διδάσκω	_____	σῴζω	_____
ἐγείρω	_____		

8. Some verbs are deponent only in the future and active in the present: Give the deponent future for each.

βαίνω	_____	πίνω	_____
βλέπω	_____	τίκτω	_____
γινώσκω	_____	φεύγω	_____
ἐσθίω	_____	χαίρω	_____
λαμβάνω	_____		

9. The future of ἀκούω may be its regular form _____ or the deponent formation _____ .

10. The future of these deponent verbs is formed differently:

ἀποκρίνομαι _____

ἔρχομαι _____

γίνομαι _____

11. Future of the Verb εἰμί. Complete the conjugation in the future.

ἔσ_____	I shall be	_____	We shall be
_____	thou shall be	_____	ye (all) shall be
_____	he, she, or it shall be.	_____	they shall be

12. The Adjectives μέγας, πολύς. Complete the declensions, noting the irregularities in formation: Giving the accent marks is part of it.

	M.	F.	N.	M.	F.	N.
N.	μέγα___	μεγαλ___	μεγ___	μεγαλ___	μεγαλ___	μεγαλ___
G.	μεγαλ___	μεγαλ___	μεγαλ___	μεγαλ___	μεγαλ___	μεγαλ___
D.	μεγαλ___	μεγαλ___	μεγαλ___	μεγαλ___	μεγαλ___	μεγαλ___
A.	μεγ___	μεγαλ___	μεγ___	μεγαλ___	μεγαλ___	μεγαλ___
V.	μεγ___	μεγαλ___	μεγ___	μεγαλ___	μεγαλ___	μεγαλ___

Complete and read aloud the declensions for both μέγας and πολύς.

	Singular			**Plural**		
	M.	**F.**	**N.**	**M.**	**F.**	**N.**
N.	πολ___	πολλ___	πολ___	πολλ___	πολλ___	πολλ___
G.	πολλ___	πολλ___	πολλ___	πολλ___	πολλ___	πολλ___
D.	πολλ___	πολλ___	πολλ___	πολλ___	πολλ___	πολλ___
A.	πολ___	πολλ___	πολ___	πολλ___	πολλ___	πολλ___
V.	πολ___	πολλ___	πολ___	πολλ___	πολλ___	πολλ___

Lesson 17

The Verb: First Aorist Active Indicative
The Pronoun: The Relative Pronoun

1. Distinctive Features of the First Aorist Active Indicative. The imperfect expresses _____ or _____ action in the past. ἔγραφον means ___ _____ _____, or ___ _____ ___ _____. While the aorist is ἔγραψα, ___ _____. "I have written" (perfect tense) will be explained later and will not be used for the aorist.

2. The "first" and "second" aorist have the same time element, but are _____ in **different** ways.

3. The first aorist is conjugated in three ways.

(i) Like the future, a ____ is added to the stem. Combining consonants with the **σ** is done by following the basic rules:

___, ___, ___ + **σ** = **ψ** (ps)   ___, ___, ___ + **σ** = **ξ** (ks)   ___, ___, ___ + **σ** = **σ**

γράφω = ___γρα_____   βαπτίζω = ___βάπ_____
κηρύσσω = ___κήρυ_____   κρύπτω = ___κρυ_____
πείθω = ___πει_____   διώκω = ___δίω_____

(ii) Write the endings for the imperfect and first aorist:

Imperfect		First Aorist	
-_____	-_____	-_____	-_____
-_____	-_____	-_____	-_____
-_____	-_____	-_____	-_____

(iii) The aorist (takes/does not take) an augment.

4. Give the conjugation of the first aorist indicative active with accents and breathing marks:

___λυ____   ___λύ_____
___λυ____   ___λύ_____
___λυ____   ___λύ_____

5. Give the 1st aorist irregular formations for the following:

ἁμαρτάνω _____ διδάσκω _____ φέρω _____

βλαστάνω _____ κλαίω _____

δεικνύω _____ κράζω _____

6. The Relative Pronoun. Define the following grammatical terms: Relative Pronoun – _____. Antecedent – _____. If the antecedent is not expressed, the relative pronoun ___ (in any case or number) has the meaning "_____," or "that one who." ὃς οὐ λαμβάνει. . . : "_____ *does not take*. . . ."

7. Decline the relative pronoun noting that the endings are the same as the first-second declension adjectives except for the _____ in the neuter nominative and accusative singular:

	Singular			Plural		
	M.	**F.**	**N.**	**M.**	**F.**	**N.**
N.	____	____	____	____	____	____
G.	____	____	____	____	____	____
D.	____	____	____	____	____	____
A.	____	____	____	____	____	____

8. The relative pronoun agrees with its _____ in gender and number, but not necessarily in _____. The form of the pronoun will usually be in the nominative case if it is the _____; in the accusative case if it is the _____ _____, or in the dative case if it is the _____ _____.

9. Sometimes the relative pronoun is "attracted" by the case of its _____ and may not be placed in the same case as its function in the dependent clause.

10. The relative pronoun may be used as a _____ pronoun in a distributive sense, as in: ὃς μὲν . . . ὃς δὲ: "_____ . . . _____."

Lesson

18

The Verb: The Second Aorist Active Indicative
Indirect Speech

1. Distinctive Features of the Second Aorist Active Indicative. A change takes place within the _____ of the verb or a _____ stem is used. Normally in English-____ is added to a verb to make it past tense: "I walk, _____." Sometimes a different stem is used: "I go – _____" (English).

2. A few verbs have both a first and second aorist: ἁμαρτάνω – _____;
_____.

3. The second aorist also takes an _____.

4. Write the second aorist of βάλλω with accents:

_____ _____   The imperfect stem is βαλλ- (ἔβαλλον).
_____ _____   The aorist stem is βαλ- (ἔβαλον).
_____ _____

5. Write the second aorist for these verbs: These verbs are conjugated with the regular endings of the imperfect.

ἄγω	_____	ἐσθίω	_____	μανθάνω	_____
ἁμαρτάνω	_____	εὑρίσκω	_____	πάσχω	_____
ἀποθνήσκω	_____	ἔχω	_____	πίνω	_____
βάλλω	_____	λαμβάνω	_____	πίπτω	_____
βλέπω *	_____	λέγω	_____	τίκτω	_____
ἔρχομαι	_____	λείπω	_____	φεύγω	_____

*It uses the second aorist of the verb ὁράω.

6. These verbs do not have the identical endings of the imperfect. Complete the paradigm:

	γινώσκω			**βαίνω**	
ἔγν	___	ἔγν_____	ἔβ___	ἐβ_____	
ἔγν	___	ἔγν_____	ἔβ___	ἐβ_____	
ἔγν	___	ἔγν_____	ἔβ___	ἐβ_____	

φέρω has a first aorist formed on a different stem: _____-.

47

The second aorist has the same stem to which the _____ active endings are added: ἔνεγκον, -κες, -κε, -κομεν, -κετε, -κον.

7. βλέπω, ἔρχομαι, and λέγω may have first aorist endings.

εἶδ_____   ἐξῆλθ_____   εἶπ_____

8. Indirect Speech. The actual words of the speaker is "_____ speech" (set off by inverted commas, "single quotes"). When a report is given, no quotes are used. This is called "_____ speech."

9. Two ways of constructing indirect speech are: (i) by putting the _____ clause in the infinitive, or (ii) by using _____ to introduce the dependent sentence.

10. In Greek, the same tense is used that was used in the _____ speech. Examples: ἡ οὖν Μάρθα ὡς ἤκουσεν (past) ὅτι Ἰησοῦς ἔρχεται (present) —"*when Martha heard that Jesus is coming.*" (In English the correct form of the dependent sentence is "*that Jesus* **was coming**.") Explain the reason for the tense of ἤκουσεν and ἔρχεται:

_____

_____

_____

_____

Lesson
19

1. Distinctive Features of the Aorist Middle Indicative. Complete the conjugation of aorist indicative middle:

ἐ-λυ-___-_____*   ἐ-λυ___-_____
ἐ-λύ-___-_____   ἐ-λύ___-_____
ἐ-λύ-___-_____   ἐ-λύ___-_____

           * "I loosed for myself."

The rule of combining consonants applies here also:

__, __, __ + σ = ψ (ps);   __, __, __ + σ = ξ(ks);   __, __, __ + σ = σ

ἄρχομαι _____ ἅπτομαι _____

2. The largest number of verbs which have an aorist in the middle voice are _____ verbs.

3. Certain verbs, such as γίνομαι and λείπομαι, have developed certain changes within the stem in the aorist:

ἐγεν_____   ἐγεν_____   ἐλιπ_____   ἐλιπ_____
ἐγέν_____   ἐγέν_____   ἐλίπ_____   ἐλίπ_____
ἐγέν_____   ἐγέν_____   ἐλίπ_____   ἐλίπ_____

ἔρχομαι forms the second aorist (on a different stem using imperfect active endings): The aorist of ἔρχομαι is : _____.

4. Distinctive Features of the Aorist Passive Indicative. The combination ___, a characteristic of the future passive, is used. The aorist passive (has/does not have) the augment.

Complete the conjugation of aorist indicative passive, and give accent and breathing marks:

__-λύ-___-_____   __-λύ___-_____
__-λύ-___-_____   __-λύ___-_____
__-λύ-___-_____   __-λύ___-_____

5. The passive aorist form of γίνομαι as a deponent verb is _____. The middle and passive of ἀποκρίνομαι are _____ and _____. The passive aorist of πορεύομαι is _____.

6. Write the aorist passive with accent and breathing marks for the following:

ἄγω _____   ἀποκαλύπτω _____
βαπτίζω _____   πείθω _____
πράσσω _____

7. Certain verbs form the aorist passive:

(i) By dropping the **θ**: thus γράφω becomes _____ (no **θ**).

(ii) By inserting a **σ** between the stem and the regular ending, if their stem ends in a long vowel; thus ἀκούω becomes _____ (**σ** added), κλείω _____.

The preceding rule (**σ** added). does not, however, apply to all verbs whose stem ends in a vowel: e.g. λύω _____.

(iii) By effecting changes within the stem or by using a different stem.

Give the aorist passive form of the following:

ἀνοίγω   (has a regular passive form as well as 3 irregular forms).

ἀνοίγω _____ also _____

_____   _____

βλέπω _____
γινώσκω _____
δεικνύω _____
διδάσκω _____
εὑρίσκω _____
κρύπτω _____
λαμβάνω _____
λέγω _____
στρέφω _____
σῴζω _____
τίκτω _____
φέρω _____

Note: No liquid/nasal verbs were included above.

Lesson 20

The Contract Verbs: Present and Imperfect Active, Middle and Passive

1. The Contract Verbs. General Rules. Give the endings of the three groups of contract verbs -_____, -_____, and -_____ verbs. (In contract verbs, two vowels produce one _____ vowel, or a _____.)

2. Using the rules you have learned give the contractions observing correct accent:

(i) **-αω** verbs

α + ο, ω or ου = _____   τιμά+ομεν = τιμ_____
                                τιμά+ουσι = τιμ_____

α + ε or η = _____   τιμά+ετε, -ητε = τιμ_____

α + ει or η = _____   τιμά+ει, -άη = τιμ_____
                                τιμά+ειν = τιμᾶν_____

Exception: The present infinitive active

(ii) **-εω** verbs

ε + ε = _____   φιλέ+ετε = φιλ _____
ε + ο = _____   φιλέ+ομεν = φιλ _____
ε + long vowel or diphthong = the original long vowel or diphthong. (The ε is _____.)

φιλέ+ω = φιλ_____   φιλέ+ουσι = φιλ_____

(iii) **-οω** verbs

ο + short vowel (or **ου**) = _____   δηλό+ετε = δηλ_____
                                          δηλό+ουσι = δηλ_____

ο + long vowel = _____   δηλό+ω = δηλ_____

ο + diphthong containing **ι**
or a vowel with a subscript = ___.   δηλό+ει, +η = δηλ_____

Exception (Infinitive)   δηλό+ειν = _____

3. Complete the conjugation with accent:

Present Active

τιμά-ω	τιμ____	φιλέ-ω	φιλ____	δηλό-ω	δηλ____
τιμά-εις	τιμ____	φιλέ-εις	φιλ____	δηλό-εις	δηλ____
τιμά-ει	τιμ____	φιλέ-ει	φιλ____	δηλό-ει	δηλ____
τιμά-ομεν	τιμ____	φιλέ-ομεν	φιλ____	δηλό-ομεν	δηλ____
τιμά-ετε	τιμ____	φιλέ-ετε	φιλ____	δηλό-ετε	δηλ____
τιμά-ουσι(ν)	τιμ____(ν)	φιλέ-ουσι(ν)	φιλ____(ν)	δηλό-ουσι(ν)	δηλ____(ν)

Imperfect Active

ἐτίμα-ον	ἐτίμ____	ἐφίλε-ον	ἐφίλ____	ἐδήλο-ον	ἐδήλ____
ἐτίμα-ες	ἐτίμ____	ἐφίλε-ες	ἐφίλ____	ἐδήλο-ες	ἐδήλ____
ἐτίμα-ε	ἐτίμ____	ἐφίλε-ε	ἐφίλ____	ἐδήλο-ε	ἐδήλ____
ἐτίμά-ομεν	ἐτίμ____	ἐφιλέ-ομεν	ἐφιλ____	ἐδηλό-ομεν	ἐδηλ____
ἐτίμά-ετε	ἐτίμ____	ἐφιλέ-ετε	ἐφιλ____	ἐδηλό-ετε	ἐδηλ____
ἐτίμα-ον	ἐτίμ____	ἐφίλε-ον	ἐφίλ____	ἐδήλο-ον	ἐδηλ____

Present Middle/Passive

τιμά-ομαι	τιμ____	φιλέ-ομαι	φιλ____	δηλό-ομαι	δηλ____
τιμά-η	τιμ____	φιλέ-η	φιλ____	δηλό-η	δηλ____
τιμά-εται	τιμ____	φιλέ-εται	φιλ____	δηλό-εται	δηλ____
τιμα-όμεθα	τιμ____	φιλε-όμεθα	φιλ____	δηλο-όμεθα	δηλ____
τιμά-εσθε	τιμ____	φιλέ-εσθε	φιλ____	δηλό-εσθε	δηλ____
τιμά-ονται	τιμ____	φιλέ-ονται	φιλ____	δηλό-ονται	δηλ____

Imperfect Middle/Passive

ἐτιμα-όμην	ἐτιμ____	ἐφιλε-όμην	ἐφιλ____	ἐδηλο-όμην	ἐδηλ____
ἐτιμά-ου	ἐτιμ____	ἐφιλέ-ου	ἐφιλ____	ἐδηλό-ου	ἐδηλ____
ἐτιμά-ετο	ἐτιμ____	ἐφιλέ-ετο	ἐφιλ____	ἐδηλό-ετο	ἐδηλ____
ἐτιμα-όμεθα	ἐτιμ____	ἐφιλε-όμεθα	ἐφιλ____	ἐδηλο-όμεθα	ἐδηλ____
ἐτιμά-εσθε	ἐτιμ____	ἐφιλέ-εσθε	ἐφιλ____	ἐδηλό-εσθε	ἐδηλ____
ἐτιμά-οντο	ἐτιμ____	ἐφιλέ-οντο	ἐφιλ____	ἐδηλό-οντο	ἐδηλ____

4. Contraction takes place only when the ending begins with a _____, and only in the _____ and _____ tenses.

5. The **α** of the stem in the **αω** verbs, with either **ει** or **η** of the regular endings of the verbs resulting in **ᾳ**, is a source of possible confusion in that the 3rd person singular present indicative active and the 2nd person singular present middle/passive of the same mood are identical in their contracted forms: τιμά + ει = _____; τιμά + η = _____.

6. Rules of accent may not be violated in accenting contract verbs. If the accent would fall on one of the uncontracted syllables, the accent is always placed on the _____ syllable.

7. In the vocabularies the uncontracted forms are given. Explain why this is so:

_____

_____

The Contract Verbs: Future and Aorist Indicative
The Verb ζάω
The Adjective: Contract Adjectives

1. Contract Verbs. Future and Aorist Indicative. Other than in the present and imperfect, contract verbs take _____ endings in the other tenses. Complete the paradigm with accents:

Fut. Act.	Aor. Act.
τιμ_____	_τίμ_____
φιλ_____	_φίλ_____
δηλ_____	_δήλ_____

Fut. Pass.	Aor. Pass.
τιμ_____	ἐτιμ_____
φιλ_____	ἐφιλ_____
δηλ_____	ἐδηλ_____

2. The two exceptions are:

(i) In the **-αω** group the ___ is retained if it is preceded by ε, ι, or ϱ; also in πεινάω and κλάω. Complete the paradigm with accents:

ἰάομαι	_____	πεινάω	_____
θεάομαι	_____	κλάω	_____
καταράομαι	_____		

(ii) In the **-εω** group, the verb καλέω retains the ε before ____ in the future and aorist active (καλέσω and _____), but turns into ___ before the **θ** of this tense in the passive (κληθήσομαι, _____).

The future and aorist passive of καλέω are formed on the stem **κλ-**. The verb τελέω, retains the ___ in all tenses, the future and aorist passive inserts a ___ between the stem and the ending. Thus (f.a.) τελ____, (a.a.) ἐτέλ____, (f.p.) τελε_____, (a.p.) ἐτελ_____.

The **ε** contract vowel of the verb δοκέω does not show up at all in the future and aorist. Give the future and aorist form. _____ _____.

3. The Verb ζάω is slightly _____ (contract verb): Fill in the paradigm with accent:

Present	Indicative		Imperfect	
ζῶ	_____		_____	_____
_____	_____		_____	_____
_____	_____		_____	_____

The future deponent: _____ (rarely ζήσω)

4. Contract Adjectives. There are a small number of adjectives of the first-second declension with a stem ending in ε- to which contraction takes place. Give the English translation for the following:

χρυσοῦς _____   διπλοῦς _____

ἀργυροῦς _____   τετραπλοῦς _____

ἁπλοῦς _____ or _____

Complete the following with accents:

	M.	F.	N.
N.V.	ἁπλ_____	ἁπλ_____	ἁπλ_____
G.	ἁπλ_____	ἁπλ_____	ἁπλ_____
D.	ἁπλ_____	ἁπλ_____	ἁπλ_____
A.	ἁπλ_____	ἁπλ_____	ἁπλ_____

	M.	F.	N.
N.V.	ἁπλ_____	ἁπλ_____	ἁπλ_____
G.	ἁπλ_____	ἁπλ_____	ἁπλ_____
D.	ἁπλ_____	ἁπλ_____	ἁπλ_____
A.	ἁπλ_____	ἁπλ_____	ἁπλ_____

Lesson 22

Liquid and Nasal Verbs: Future and Aorist Indicative
The Pronoun: The Possessive Pronoun

1. Liquid and Nasal Verbs. The liquid consonants are ____, ____, and the nasal consonants are _____, _____. When a verb ends in one of these consonants, a peculiarity occurs in the formation of the _____ and _____ tenses in all three voices.

2. Future Active and Middle.

(i) The ___ is dropped in this tense.

(ii) Note the conjugation is like the contract verb of the -εω group. Accent determines the way to tell the _____ active from the _____ active: μένω (present) and μενῶ (future).

(iii) The verbal stem is used if it differs from the _____ stem. Thus αἴρω = _____, _____. ἀποστέλλω = _____, _____.

3. The stem used for the future of λέγω is _____-. Complete the paradigm with accents:

Future Active: ἐρ_____   ἐρ_____
ἐρ_____   ἐρ_____
ἐρ_____   ἐρ_____

4. ἀποθνήσκω and πίπτω are deponent only in the future. The verbal stems -_____ and πεσ. Again the -εω group is used for the conjugation. These are in the NT: ἀποθαν_____(3d pers. sing.), ἀποθαν_____ (2d pers. pl.), πεσ_____ (1st pers. sing.), πεσ_____ (3d pers. sing), πεσ_____ (3d pers. pl.).

5. Aorist Active and Middle. These are formed as follows:

(i) The **σ** is _____ and normal endings are used.
(ii) The augment is _____.
(iii) A change is sometimes made in the verbal _____ by lengthening it. ἀναγγέλλω = _____; αἴρω = _____.

The verb βάλλω uses the second aorist ending: _____.

6. Future and Aorist Passive.

The normal endings of these tenses are added to the verbal stem, some nasal verbs drop the **ν**. Give the future passive of the verb κρίνω – _____ (future passive), _____ (aorist passive).

The liquid verbs retain the **λ** or **ρ**. Thus ἐγείρω becomes _____ (aorist passive).

7. Complete this chart for future reference:

Present Active	Future Active	Future MiddlePassive	Future Active	Aorist Passive	Aorist
ἀγγέλλω	_____			ἤγγειλα	ἠγγέλην
αἴρω	ἀρῶ		_____	ἦρα	ἤρθην
ἀνατέλλω				ἀνέτειλα	
ἀποκρίνομαι					ἀπεκρίθην
ἀποκτείνω	ἀποκτενῶ			ἀπέκτεινα	_____
βάλλω	βαλῶ	βληθήσομαι		ἔβαλον	
ἐγείρω	ἐγερῶ	ἐγερθήσομαι		_____	ἠγέρθην
κρίνω	κρινῶ		_____	ἔκρινα	ἐκρίθην
μένω	μενῶ			ἔμεινα	
ξηραίνω				ἐξήρανα	ἐξηράνθην
ποιμαίνω	_____		ἐποίμανα		
σπείρω				ἔσπειρα	_____
στέλλω	στελῶ			_____	ἐστάλην
φαίνω		_____		ἐφάνην	
		or _____			
χαίρω			_____		ἐχάρην

Notice the verbs (ἀν-, ἀπ-), ἀγγέλλω, σπείρω, (ἀπο) στέλλω, φαίνω and χαίρω form the passive aorist as a 2d aorist drop the ____.

8. The Possessive Pronoun. τὸ βιβλίον μου: shows the possession by using the _____ of the personal pronoun. For emphatic force, the possessive pronoun is used: τὸ _____ βιβλίον.

9. The possessive pronoun is declined on the pattern of the _____ and _____ declension _____, and agrees in _____, _____, and _____ with the noun it qualifies. Only in the first and second persons is the possessive pronoun found.

10. Give the nominative (N.) possessive pronouns with accents:

(N.) 1st person singular: _____, _____, _____
(N.) 1st person plural: _____, _____, _____
(N.) 2nd person singular: _____, _____, _____
(N.) 2nd person plural: _____, _____, _____

11. The possessive pronoun can be used in the _____, or in the _____ sense. Translate:

ὁ ἐμὸς δοῦλος "_____ _____."

ἐμός ἐστιν ὁ δοῦλος "____ _____ ____ _____."

Lesson

23

The Noun:
The Third Declension:
1. Masculine and Feminine Nouns
With Stem Ending in a Consonant

1. Distinctive Features of the Third Declension Nouns. The third declension nouns present a greater difficulty, than those of the other two declensions do. Memorization is important!

2. Two basic distinctions:

(i) Between the _____ and _____ genders on the one hand and neuter nouns on the other.

(ii) Between masculine and feminine nouns whose stems end in a _____ and those whose stem ends in a _____. Most nouns in the third declension have their stems end in a _____.

3. The stem is not found by dropping the ending of the _____ singular as in first and second declensions. The _____ singular is used to determine the stem. When studying the vocabulary, learn the nominative and the genitive forms along with the gender.

4. Nouns of this declension usually have in the genitive, dative and accusative singular, and all cases of the plural _____ _____ more than the nominative singular.

5. Endings. Give the masculine and feminine endings:

	Singular	Plural
N.	(_____)	_____
G.	-_____	_____
D.	-_____	_____
A.	-_____	_____
V.	(Usually the Nom.)	_____

6. The ___ and ___ are short in the endings of this declension.

7. Masculine and Feminine Nouns with a Stem Ending in a Consonant. These end in a labial, guttural (and **κτ**), or dental and form the nominative singular by adding the ς to the stem. Give the nominative singular with accents for the following:

λαιλαπ + ς _____   ἐλπιδ + ς _____
φυλακ + ς _____   ποδ + ς _____
νυκ + ς _____

61

8. Changes take place before the **σ** of the ending of the dative plural. In nouns with stem endings:

      (i) In **ϱ** the __ is retained before the **σ**, thus σωτὴϱ = _____.

      (ii) In a nasal the **ν** is dropped, thus ἡγεμὼν = _____.

      (iii) In **ντ** this is dropped and the preceding vowel is lengthened.

$$αντ+ σι = _____$$
$$εντ+ σι = _____$$
$$οντ+ σι = _____$$

Thus ἄϱχων, ἄϱχοντος, _____, (dat. plural).

9. Nouns Whose Stems End in a Dental Preceded by ι:

      (i) If they are accented on the ultima in the nominative, they form the accusative singular by adding the normal **α** ending to the normal stem thus, ἐλπίς, = _____.

      (ii) If they are accented on the penult in the nominative, they form the accusative singular by adding **ν** to a shortened stem. Thus, χάϱις = _____.

10. One-syllable nouns in the nominative singular deviate from the rule on noun accents in the genitive and dative of both numbers. The accent is not retained on the stem, but moves to the _____. Give the genitive and dative of both numbers with accents of χείϱ = _____, _____, _____ _____.

11, 12. Read aloud the declensions in these sections until the pattern for forming each noun is understood.

Lesson 24

The Third Declension Nouns:
2. Masculine and Feminine Nouns with Stem Ending in a Vowel
The Dative of Respect

1. The second group of third declension nouns is made up of _____ and _____ nouns, whose stem ends in a _____. It is made of up of _____ smaller groups.

2. The First Group: Stems Ending in a Variable Vowel. This group has a variable stem, one, which becomes ___ in the nominative, accusative, and vocative singular, and becomes an ___ for all other cases. All nouns of the group are _____ (gender) and generally abstract nouns.

3. Departures from Regular Endings:

(i) -**ος** in the genitive singular lengthens to -_____.

(ii) In the accusative singular the alternative ending is - **ν** - instead of -__.

(iii) If the **ε** of the stem is followed by **ες** in the nominative plural ending or the **ας** of the accusative plural ending a contraction results in = _____.

4. The _____ singular must also be known in this group.

5. Decline ἡ πόλις with accents:

	Singular	**Plural**
N.	_____	_____
G.	_____	_____
D.	_____	_____
A.	_____	_____
V.	_____	_____

6. The Second Group: Stems Ending in _____. All nouns in this group are _____, mainly describing those in a particular _____.

7. Departures from regular endings are:

(i) -**ος** of the genitive singular lengthens to -____. However, the **εω** in the genitives of this group is not considered as a _____ syllable.

The **εω** in both genitives is considered as a single syllable diphthong.

(ii) υ of the stem is dropped when followed by a _____ ending. A contraction takes place in the accusative plural between the ε of the stem and the α of the regular ending -ας resulting in ____. The nominative singular is formed by adding ____ to the stem.

8. Notice the similarity of endings in the plural. The _____, accusative and _____, plural in both groups have the same endings.

9. Read aloud three times the declension of ὁ ἱερεύς.

10. The Third Group: Stems Ending in ____. This small group has both _____ and _____ nouns. These nouns are declined similarly to the first group. The most distinctive feature of this small group is the diaresis which in the dative singular marks it as a _____ syllable. Notice that the υ sometimes drops out of the _____ diphthong in the genitive singular of the word **νοῦς**.

11. Complete the declensions:

Singular	**Plural**
N. ὁ ἰχθύ____	οἱ ἰχθύ____
G. ἰχθύ____	ἰχθύ____
D. ἰχθύ____	ἰχθύ____
A. ἰχθύ____	ἰχθύ____
V. ἰχθύ	ἰχθύ____

Singular	**No Plurals in the NT**
N ἡ ἰσχύ____	
G. ἰσχύ____	
D. ἰσχύ____	
A. ἰσχύ____	
V. ἰσχύ	

Singular	**Plural**
N. ὁ νο____	οἱ νό____
G. νο____	νο____
D. νο____	νο____ (ν)
A. νο____	νό____
V. νο____	νό____

12. Dative of Respect. It is used to indicate a specific relationship between various parts of speech and to define its _____. Translate: τὸν δὲ ἀσθενοῦντα τῇ πίστει προσλαμβάνεσθε: *"and welcome him who is weak so far as ____ _____ _____ _____"* (Rom. 14:1).

Lesson 25

The Third Declension Nouns:
3. Neuter Nouns

1. Basically, these two groups of neuter nouns in the third declension have a _____ for their endings.

2. First Group: Stems Ending in ____. These drop the final _____ when no ending is added to the _____, _____, and vocative _____, and before the ___ of the dative _____. Give the stem endings.

	Singular	**Plural**
N.	–	-____-____
G.	-____-____	-____-____
D.	-____-____	-____-____ (_)
A.	–	-____-____
V.	–	-____-____

5. Second Group. Stems Ending in -____. Whenever the ending begins with a vowel the ___ is dropped and a contraction takes place between the remaining ___ of the stem and the vowel of the ending (the dative plural being the exception). In the nominative, accusative, and vocative _____, the ___ is turned into **o** and the ___ is retained.

6. Give the declension of the second group:

	Singular	**Plural**
N.	-____	-____ (___) ___:___
G.	-___ (___) ___ ___	-____ (___) ___:___
D.	-___ (___) ___ ___	-____ (___)
A.	-____	-____ (___) ___:___
V.	-____	-____ (___) ___:___

7. Two nouns πῦρ and ὄρος are irregular in one form of their declension. Complete the following:

πῦρ (dat. sing.), _____ (fire).

ὄρος (gen. pl.), _____ (mountain);

65

Lesson 26

The Verb: Perfect and Pluperfect Indicative

1. Perfect and Pluperfect: Their Meanings.

(i) The perfect tense denotes an action in the past with its effects _____ _____. The perfect emphasizes the _____ of the action. The perfect is a past and present tense.

(ii) The _____ views the effects as existing at a certain time in the past, or _____ to another event expressed or implied in the text.

2. Formation of the Perfect.

In all three voices there is "_____." This consists of _____ _____ consonant followed by _____ and prefixed to the stem: λύω– ____λυκα. In compound verbs, the reduplication is prefixed to the _____.

3. Certain verbs depart from the pattern of reduplication in the following ways:

(i) The initial vowel or diphthong is lengthened. ἐλπίζω, _____; οἰκοδομέω, _____.

(ii) Verbs beginning with **θ**, **φ**, **χ**, receive the hard consonants thus **θ** = __; **φ** = __; **χ** = __. θεραπεύω, ___θεράπευκα; φανερόω, ___φανέρωμαι; χαρίζομαι, ___χάρισμαι.

(iii) In verbs beginning with **ζ** and **ξ**, by prefixing _____. Thus ζητέω, ___ζήτηκα; ξηραίνω, ___ξήραμμαι.

(iv) In verbs beginning with _____ consonants
(a) Generally, by prefixing ___σταυρόω, ___σταύρωμαι.
(b) If the second consonant is a liquid or nasal (__ __ __), the reduplication is built on the first consonant as if it were the only one. Give the proper reduplication: γράφω __γραφα; θνήσκω ___θνηκα; πληρόω ___πλήρωκα; χρηματίζω ___χρημάτισμαι.

4. Perfect Active.

Conjugate λύω in the perfect indicative active with accents:

____-λυ-____   ____-λύ_____
____-λυ-____   ____-λύ_____
____-λυ-____   ____-λύ_____ or ____-λυ_____

5. If the stem ends in a dental or a __, these are dropped. Thus: ἐλπίζω = (ἐλπιδ−)
_____, κρίνω− _____.

6. Some verbs which have a second perfect, are formed by omitting the ___. Thus,
γράφω becomes _____.

7. Perfect Middle and Passive. The endings are the same as those of the present passive, except the initial vowel (or connecting vowel) of the ending is _____; and the second person singular ending is _____. Complete this paradigm:

λέ-λυ_____	λε-λύ_____
λέ-λυ_____	λέ-λυ_____
λέ-λυ_____	λέ-λυ_____

8. The short vowel in the contract verb stem endings will lengthen before the ____ of the perfect active and the _____ endings of the middle and passive, just as it did before the ___ of the future and the _____. Fill in the proper forms with accents:

	τιμάω	φιλέω	δηλόω
perfect active	_____	_____	_____
perfect passive	_____	_____	_____

9. When the stem ends in certain consonants these undergo a change in the perfect or aorist passive. Write the changes for certain consonants:

(i) For the gutturals, __, ___, ____.
Any guttural before "**μ**" becomes ___, thus δέχομαι = δέδε___μαι
Any guttural before "**τ**" becomes ___, thus ἄγω = ἦ___ται
Any guttural before "**θ**" becomes ___, thus ἄγω = ἤ___θη

(ii) For the labials, __, ___, ____.
Any labials before "**μ**" becomes ___, thus γράφω = γέγρα___μαι.
Any labials before "**τ**" becomes ___ ,thus γράφω = γέγρα___ται

(iii) For the dentals, ___, ___, ___.
Any dental before "**μ** or **τ**" becomes ___, thus ἑτοιμάζω= ἡτοί _____ μαι; or ἡτοίμα___ται.
Any dental before "**κ** or **σ**" is _____, thus βαπτίζω = becomes (perfect active is) βεβάπτι____.

(iv) The nasal ___ before **κ, μ, σ, τ** is usually dropped, thus κρίνω = becomes (perfect active is) _____, but ξηραίνω is _____. Sometimes the "**ν**" is retained and ___ is inserted between this and the ending: μένω becomes (perfect active) _____.

In applying these changes where the verbal stem is different from the present stem one should remember the other rules:

	Stem	Original Stem
	-σσ	- _____
	-ζ	- _____
	-ττ	- _____

10. No verb with a stem ending in a _____ occurs in the perfect middle or passive indicative second person singular or plural, or a third person plural ending. Thus, we need not be concerned with what happened with the consonantal stem with the **σ** or ___ ending.

11. Irregular Perfect Formations. Read aloud this section carefully in the textbook. Pronounce the "ω" verb and the following verb(s) for each word. These may need to be read aloud more than once in order to comprehend how the verbs are formed.

12. Formation of the Pluperfect Active and Passive. This tense takes the reduplication preceded by the augment (occasionally omitted). Whereas the *perfect* active is characterized by – ___ endings, the *pluperfect* active is characterized by – ___ endings.

Complete the paradigm with correct breathing marks and accents:

Active	Middle and Passive
___-___-λύ_____	___-___-λύ-_____
___-___-λύ_____	___-___-λυ-_____
___-___-λύ_____	___-___-λυ-_____
___-___-λύ_____	___-___-λύ-_____
___-___-λύ_____	___-___-λυ-_____
___-___-λύ_____	___-___-λυ-_____

13. Principal Parts. It is necessary for one to master the six principal parts of a Greek verb. Complete the following by naming the other five tenses and the Greek. You may abbreviate.

Present Act.   _____; _____; _____; _____; _____
λύω   _____; _____; _____; _____; _____

Lesson 27

The Participle:
1. General Rules. Active Voice
The Verb οἶδα

1. General Rules Governing the Participle. The participle has the nature of both the
_____ and the _____. As a verb, the participle has _____,
_____, and may have an _____. As an adjective it is declined, and must
_____ in _____, _____, and _____ with the noun or pronoun it
qualifies. Depending on the role it plays in a sentence, a participle is adjectival or
_____.

2. Fill in the proper participial form with any **articles** necessary and translate for the
following uses:

(i) As an attributive adjective: "ὁ μαθητὴς _____ τὸν κύριον."
(The disciple _____ _____ the Lord.)

(ii) As a noun (in the nominative singular masculine): "_____ _____
τὸν κύριον" (_____ the Lord).

(iii) As a noun (in the nominative plural, masculine): _____ τὸν
κύριον. (_____ the Lord.)

The participle is used as a noun: _____ (nom.) τὸν κύριον:
(_____) _____ see the Lord.

The attributive participle should be treated by using the _____ pronoun
(ὅς).

3. The adverbial participle may answer the questions: "_____," "_____," or
"_____" the action of the verb took place. It is (never/always) preceded by the article. Give three possible translations for the phrase to reflect the ideas indicated. ὁ
μαθητὴς βλέπων τὸν κύριον.

(time) _____
(cause) _____
(manner)_____

Also, the "_____ participle" may be used to explain that the action was
done in spite of circumstances. The "_____ participle" is a hebraism: "εὐλογῶν
(nom.) εὐλογήσω σε." (I will bless thee _____.) Finish the sentences to
reflect the translations.

"ὁ διδάσκαλος _____ ἐν ταύτῃ τῇ οἰκίᾳ ἐκήρυσσεν": (the teacher, while he was remaining in this house, was preaching). "ὁ διδάσκαλος _____ _____ ἐν ταύτῃ τῇ οἰκίᾳ ἐκήρυσσεν": (The teacher, <u>who was remaining</u> in this house, was preaching.)

4. The Time Element of the Adjectival Participles. There (is a/is no) time element at all in the present and aorist indicative participles when they are used as a noun or as an adjective. The difference between present and aorist participles is the aspect of _____ or _____ action.

5. The Time Element of the Adverbial Participles. This depends on the action of the _____ verb.

      (i) In the present, the action is _____ to that of the principal verb.
      (ii) In the future, action is _____ to that of the principal verb.
      (iii) In the aorist the action is _____ that of the principal verb.

6. The Participle in the Active Voice. The stem for the present active participle is λυοντ–. The masculine and neuter are declined like nouns of the _____ declension (e.g. ἄρχων). The feminine gender adds a –σ to the stem (with the ____ dropping out before the σ, and the **o** lengthening to ____ as in the masculine dative plural). The feminine is patterned after the _____ declension nouns of the ____ group with stems ending in σ. Complete the following paradigm with accents:

	Masculine	Feminine	Neuter
		Singular	
N.V.	λύ_____	λύ_____	λῦ_____
G.	λύ_____	λυ_____	λύ_____
D.	λύ_____	λυ_____	λύ_____
A.	λύ_____	λύ_____	λῦ_____
		Plural	
N.V.	λύ_____	λύ_____	λύ_____
G.	λυ_____	λυ_____	λυ_____
D.	λύ_____	λυ_____	λύ_____
A.	λύ_____	λυ_____	λύ_____

7. Participles of contract verbs (follow/do not follow) the rules of contraction. Give the nom., sing. for the present act. part. for the following participles in the pattern of λύων, λύουσα, λύον, placing proper accents.

	Masculine	Feminine	Neuter
α contract	τιμ_____	τιμ_____	τιμ_____
ε contract	φιλ_____	φιλ_____	φιλ_____
o contract	δηλ_____	δηλ_____	δηλ_____

8. The future is formed by placing ____ between the stem and endings of the _____ participle. Complete the following:

	Masculine	**Feminine**	**Neuter**
		Singular	
N.V.	λύ___ων	λύ___ουσα	λῦ___ον
G.	λύ___οντος	λυ___ούσης	λύ___οντος
D.	λύ___οντι	λυ___ούσῃ	λύ___οντι
A.	λύ___οντα	λύ___ουσαν	λῦ___ον
		Plural	
N.V.	λύ___οντες	λύ___ουσαι	λύ___οντα
G.	λυ___όντων	λυ___ουσῶν	λυ___ώντων
D.	λύ___ουσι(ν)	λυ___ούσαις	λύ___ουσι(ν)
A.	λύ___οντας	λυ___ούσας	λύ___οντα

In verbs with stems that end in liquid or nasal consonants, the rule governing them in the indicative mood (**22 § 2**) applies in the participles of the future active and middle voices. In the following examples, the masculine has been given. You are to fill in the feminine and the neuter:

(M.) ἀποστελῶν,   (F.) _____,   (N.) _____
(M.) κρινῶν,   (F.) _____,   (N.) _____

9. The first aorist is formed by inserting ___ between the stem and the endings of the present and substituting **α** for **o** or **ου** sounds at the head of the ending in all three genders and in all cases. In the nominative and vocative singular of the masculine the final ___ is turned into **ς**. (Note the aorist is formed without the augment). Complete the following with correct accent:

	Masculine	**Feminine**	**Neuter**
		Singular	
N.V.	λυ_____	λυ_____	λυ_____
G.	λυ_____	λυ_____	λυ_____
D.	λυ_____	λυ_____	λυ_____
A.	λυ_____	λυ_____	λυ_____
		Plural	
N.V.	λυ_____	λυ_____	λυ_____
G.	λυ_____	λυ_____	λυ_____
D.	λυ_____	λυ_____	λυ_____
A.	λυ_____	λυ_____	λυ_____

In verbs with stems which end in liquid or nasal consonants (λ, μ, ν, ϱ) the same rule applies which governs this tense in the indicative mood (See Grammar Book Lesson 22, paragraph 5, subpoints i, iii). Thus, ἀποστείλας, κρίνας.

The _____ aorist is formed by adding the endings of the present participle to the stem of this tense, and moving the accent one syllable to the _____. Complete and place the correct accent.

$$\text{ἄγω} = \text{ἀγαγ}\_\_\_, \text{ἀγαγ}\_\_\_\_\_, \text{ἀγαγ}\_\_\_\_\_.$$
$$\text{βλέπω} = \text{ἰδ}\_\_\_\_, \text{ἰδ}\_\_\_\_\_, \text{ἰδ}\_\_\_\_\_.$$
$$\text{ἔρχομαι} = \text{ἐλθ}\_\_\_\_, \text{ἐλθ}\_\_\_\_\_, \text{ἐλθ}\_\_\_\_\_.$$

The aorist participle has (a/no) augment, this being the exclusive characteristic of the _____ mood.

10. The perfect is formed in the masculine and neuter on the general pattern of the _____ declension noun (similar to neuter nouns with stems ending in –ατ) and in the feminine on the pattern of the _____ declension noun of the ____ group with stems ending in a vowel or ____. The reduplication (is/is not) retained in all moods. Complete the following with correct accent:

Masculine	Feminine	Neuter
	Singular	
N.V.____λυ_____	____λυ_____	____λυ_____
G. ____λυ_____	____λυ_____	____λυ_____
D. ____λυ_____	____λυ_____	____λυ_____
A. ____λυ_____	____λυ_____	____λυ_____
	Plural	
N.V.____λυ_____	____λυ_____	____λυ_____
G. ____λυ_____	____λυ_____	____λυ_____
D. ____λυ_____	____λυ_____	____λυ_____
A. ____λυ_____	____λυ_____	____λυ_____

Verbs which have a second perfect retain it in the participle: Thus γέγραφα becomes _____; ἀκήκοα = _____.

11. The present participle of the verb εἰμὶ consists of the _____ _____ of the present: ____, _____, and ____.

12. The participle is negated by the use of ____.

13. Indirect Discourse. An accusative participle (with/without) an article is joined with an accusative direct object to form the equivalent of an ὅτι indirect discourse clause (Grammar: **18 § 10, i**). Indirect discourse participial phrases may be used with any verb expressing the idea of _____, _____, _____, or _____, etc.

14. Periphrastic Tenses. The periphrastic (_____-____) structure is formed by the imperfect of εἰμί preceding the present participle: Thus "καὶ _____ (imperfect of εἰμί) οἱ μαθηταὶ Ἰωάννου καὶ οἱ φαρισαῖοι νηστεύοντες": (*The disciples of John and the pharisees were fasting*). The periphrastic future is formed by the same process: "καὶ ἰδοὺ _____ (future) σιωπῶν": (*And behold, thou wilt be silent.*).

15. The Verb οἶδα. οἶδα is found only in the _____ and _____ tenses, and is used with the meaning of the present and imperfect respectively. It is conjugated in two tenses. Fill in the following paradigm with correct accent.

Indicative

Perfect		Pluperfect	
Singular	**Plural**	**Singular**	**Plural**
_____	_____	_____	_____
_____	_____	_____	_____
_____	_____	_____	_____

Give the participles: εἰδ ____ (-ότος), _____, _____

16. Like the verb οἶδα, the verb _____ is also used in the _____ tense with a present meaning.

Identify the participles on the following page.

PARSING EXERCISES

Since participles are verbal adjectives, they have case, gender and number. They also have tense and voice.

Example: λύων is a present, active, nominative, masculine, singular participle. The stem comes from the verb λύω, while the ending is masculine singular. **Know the endings** that will always identify the case, gender and number of the participles.

Know your masculine, feminine and neuter endings for participles!

Practice identifying these participles:

From (Verb)	Participle	Tense	Voice	Case	Gender	Sing./Pl.
διώκω	διωκόμενοι					
	προσευχομένου					
	δεχόμενος					
	ἐξερχομένοις					
	ἐγείροντος					
	διωκόμεναι					
	πιστεύοντες					
	γραφόμενα					
	λαμβάνοντας					
	ἄγοντες					
	ἀναβαινούσῃ					
	σῷζον					
	βαπτίζοντα					
	ὄντα					

Lesson 28

The Participle: 2. Middle and Passive Voice
Genitive Absolute
The Article: Unusual Usage of the Article

1. The Participle in the Middle and Passive Voices. In all tenses of the middle and passive voices except the aorist passive, the participle is declined like the adjective _____. The _____ and _____ genders follow the pattern of the nouns of the _____ declension. The feminine gender follows the _____ declension nouns of the ___ group. Complete the following with accents in the three genders:

Present Mid./Pass:	λυ_____,	λυ_____,	λυ_____
Future Middle:	λυ_____,	λυ_____,	λυ_____
Future Passive:	λυ_____,	λυ_____,	λυ_____
Aorist Middle:	λυ_____,	λυ_____,	λυ_____
Perfect Mid./Pass:	__λυ_____,	__λυ_____,	__λυ_____

2. The aorist passive participle is formed on the stem λυθεντ–. The aorist passive in the _____ and _____ follow the pattern of the _____ declension nouns. The _____ gender follows that of the _____ declension nouns of the ___ group and with stems ending in a **σ**. The _____ drops out before **σ**, like the present active participle, and the **ε** lengthens to ___. Notice the shift of the accent to the first syllable ending.

In the chart below, write the endings of the aorist passive participle, with correct accent.

	Singular			**Plural**		
	Masc.	**Fem.**	**Neut.**	**Masc.**	**Fem.,**	**Neut**
N.V.	λυ_____	λυ_____	λυ_____	λυ_____	λυ_____	λυ_____
G.	λυ_____	λυ_____	λυ_____	λυ_____	λυ_____	λυ_____
D.	λυ_____	λυ_____	λυ_____	λυ_____	λυ_____	λυ_____
A.	λυ_____	λυ_____	λυ_____	λυ_____	λυ_____	λυ_____

3. The second aorist middle adds the present _____ endings to the verbal stem: (remember the verbal stem may change) γίνομαι – γινόμενος (present participle) – becomes _____όμενος in the aorist middle.

In the second aorist passive the **θ** is omitted: ἀποστέλλω (present indicative) – becomes _____λείς.

77

4. Irregular formations of the aorist and perfect participles are found in the NT. Read these aloud (across the page) until they become familiar.

5. Genitive Absolute. When a noun or pronoun in the genitive case (being neither the subject, nor the object) is qualified by a participle and is separated from the main part of the sentence (independent clause), the construction is known as "_____ _____." It is a dependent clause. Consider, "ὁ ἀπόστολος θεραπεύσας τὸν τυφλὸν ἀπῆλθεν." "ὁ ἀπόστολος" is a noun qualified (modified) by the participle θεραπεύσας. "*The apostle*" is the _____ of the main verb, and since "*having healed*" modifies the subject, both are put in the nominative case—"Healing" and "coming" are done by the subject. But: "τοῦ ἀποστόλου θεραπεύσαντος τὸν τυφλὸν ὁ μαθητὴς ἀπῆλθεν" is different. "*The disciple*" (ὁ μαθητὴς), is the _____ of the principal verb, not "*the apostle*" (τοῦ ἀποστόλου). This is an example of separate actions in two different clauses. The genitive absolute is the dependent clause (incomplete thought), and the main verb and subject are in the independent clause (complete thought). "*The _____ having healed the blind man, the _____ went away*." Genitive absolutes usually occur at the _____ of the sentence as a time element.

The subject and the participle of the principal verb are put in the _____ case. (See the following pages for explanations of the participles and genitive absolute.)

6. Peculiar Usages of the Article. The article may be found preceding a preposition followed by a noun: Article + preposition + noun. The construction is a _____ phrase, and functions as an _____. "οἱ ἐν τῇ ἐκκλησίᾳ διδάσκαλοι": (the teachers who are ____ _____ _____). Translate the following phrase: "οἱ ἐν τῇ ἐκκλησίᾳ διδάσκαλοι _____ _____."

7. Quite similar is the use of an article with:

(i) An _____ as a substantive which is treated as a noun. "τοὺς ἔξω": (_____ _____ are outside).

(ii) A _____ in the genitive: "τά τοῦ κόσμου": (_____ _____ ___ the world).

The participle without the article (*temporal*, *while* or *as*):

PRESENT

Act. λύων	loosing; while loosing; as he was loosing
Mid. λυόμενος	loosing for himself; while, etc.; as, etc.
Pas. λυόμενος	being loosed; while, etc.; as, etc.

AORIST

Act. λύσας	having loosed; after he had loosed; when he had loosed
Mid. λυσάμενος	having loosed for himself; after, etc.; when, etc.

Pas. λυθείς   having been loosed; when he was loosed, when he has been, when he had been; after he was—, after he has been—; after he had been

The participle with the article (relative, [the one who, he who, or she who])

PRESENT

Act. ὁ λύων   he who looses; the man who; the one who, etc.
Mid. ὁ λυόμενος   he who looses for himself; the man who; the one who, etc
Pas. ὁ λυόμενος   he who is being loosed; the man who; the one who, etc.

AORIST

Act. ὁ λύσας   he (the man, the one) who loosed, has loosed, or had loosed
Mid. ὁ λυσάμενος   he (the man, the one) who loosed for himself; has, had, etc.
Pas. ὁ λυθείς   he (the man, the one) who was loosed; has been, had been, etc.

REMEMBER: Deponent (-ομαι) verbs will have the middle form, but will be active in meaning.

SPECIAL PRACTICE ON GENITIVE ABSOLUTES

The next few pages are designed to give you practice in recognizing genitive absolutes and distinguishing them from nominative adverbial participles. Each page has two Greek sentences.

(1) For each sentence, identify the genitive absolute if any. If there is one, write it down; otherwise, put "None."

(2) Identify the subject of the main clause.

(3) Identify the subject of the participle.

(4) Identify the case of the participle and explain why it is that case (either because it modifies the subject of the independent clause [if it is nominative], or because it modifies a subject that is different from the subject of the main clause [if it is genitive]).

(5) Translate each sentence.

An explanation of each sentence is given on the fourth page of this exercise.

1. εἰπόντων ταῦτα τῶν ἀποστόλων, οἱ μαθηταὶ ἀπῆλθον.

    (1) Gen. Abs.? _____

    (2) Subject of main clause? _____

    (3) Subject of participle? _____

    (4) Case of participle, and why? _____

    _____

    (5) Translation: _____

    _____

2. εἰπόντες ταῦτα οἱ ἀπόστολοι ἀπῆλθον.

    (1) Gen. Abs.? _____

    (2) Subject of main clause? _____

    (3) Subject of participle? _____

    (4) Case of participle, and why? _____

    _____

    (5) Translation: _____

    _____

3. λέγοντος αὐτοῦ ταῦτα οἱ μαθηταὶ ἀπῆλθον.

    (1) Gen. Abs.? _____

    (2) Subject of main clause? _____

    (3) Subject of participle? _____

    (4) Case of participle, and why? _____

    _____

    (5) Translation: _____

    _____

4. λέγων ταῦτα ἀπῆλθεν

    (1) Gen. Abs.? _____

    (2) Subject of main clause? _____

    (3) Subject of participle? _____

    (4) Case of participle, and why? _____

    _____

    (5) Translation: _____

    _____

5. οἱ μαθηταὶ διδαχθέντες ὑπὸ τοῦ κυρίου ἐξῆλθον εἰς τὴν ἔρημον.

    (1) Gen. Abs.? _____

    (2) Subject of main clause? _____

    (3) Subject of participle? _____

    (4) Case of participle, and why? _____

    _____

    (5) Translation: _____

    _____

6. τῶν μαθητῶν διδαχθέντων ὑπὸ τοῦ κυρίου ἐξῆλθον εἰς τὴν ἔρημον οἱ δοῦλοι.

    (1) Gen. Abs.? _____

    (2) Subject of main clause? _____

    (3) Subject of participle? _____

    (4) Case of participle, and why? _____

    _____

    (5) Translation: _____

    _____

EXPLANATION

1. **(a)** *(When/After) the apostles had said these things,* **(b)** *the disciples went away.*

εἰπόντων ταῦτα τῶν ἀποστόλων, οἱ μαθηταὶ ἀπῆλθον.

The genitive absolute, εἰπόντων ταῦτα τῶν ἀποστόλων, is used as the dependent clause (the incomplete thought), because its "subject" τῶν ἀποστόλων, is different from that of the independent clause (the complete thought), οἱ μαθηταὶ ἀπῆλθον. Since the participle denotes action by the apostles (rather than by the disciples), both it and its subject are in the genitive case.

2. **(a)** *When the apostles had said these things,* **(b)** *they went away.*

εἰπόντες ταῦτα οἱ ἀπόστολοι ἀπῆλθον.

Here the apostles do the action of both the dependent clause (saying these things) and the independent clause (going away). There is no genitive absolute. The participle εἰπόντες is in the nominative case because it modifies the nominative subject οἱ ἀπόστολοι of the main verb, ἀπῆλθον.

3. **(a)** *While he was saying these things,* **(b)** *the disciples went away.*

λέγοντος αὐτοῦ ταῦτα οἱ μαθηταὶ ἀπῆλθον.

The genitive absolute, λέγοντος αὐτοῦ ταῦτα, is used as the dependent clause (the incomplete thought), because its "subject" αὐτοῦ is different from that of the independent clause (the complete thought), οἱ μαθηταὶ ἀπῆλθον. Since the participle denotes action by "him" (rather than by the disciples), both it and its subject are in the genitive case.

4. *While he was saying these things, he went away.*

λέγων ταῦτα ἀπῆλθεν.

Here one person does the action both of the dependent clause (saying these things) and the independent clause (going away). Again, there is no need for a genitive absolute. The participle λέγων is in the nominative case because it modifies the nominative subject of the main verb, ἀπῆλθεν.

5. **(a)** *When the disciples had been taught by the Lord,* **(b)** *they went out into the desert.*

οἱ μαθηταὶ διδαχθέντες ὑπὸ τοῦ κυρίου ἐξῆλθον εἰς τὴν ἔρημον.

The participle in the participial phrase διδαχθέντες ὑπὸ τοῦ κυρίου is nominative because it refers to οἱ μαθηταὶ, the subject of the main clause, οἱ μαθηταὶ ἐξῆλθον εἰς τὴν ἔρημον. There is no genitive absolute.

6. **(a)** *When the disciples had been taught by the Lord,* **(b)** *the servants went out into the desert.*

τῶν μαθητῶν διδαχθέντων ὑπὸ τοῦ κυρίου ἐξῆλθον εἰς τὴν ἔρημον οἱ δοῦλοι.

Here there is a genitive absolute, τῶν μαθητῶν διδαχθέντων ὑπὸ τοῦ κυρίου, because the subject of the genitive absolute, τῶν μαθητῶν, is not the subject of the main clause, ἐξῆλθον εἰς τὴν ἔρημον οἱ δοῦλοι. Since the participle does not modify the nominative subject of the main verb (i.e., the slaves are not the ones being taught), both it and its "subject" are in the genitive case.

REMEMBER that the genitive absolute may be used if the <u>noun</u> or <u>pronoun</u> going with the participle is <u>different</u> from the <u>subject</u> of the finite (leading) verb.

Lesson
29

1. Adjectives of the Third Declension. These are in _____ groups.
The masculine and feminine use (different/the same) endings so only two endings are given in the vocabulary.

2. First Group. These adjectives have a stem ending in _____. The article (is/is not) used in vocabulary listings. Decline (with accents) ἀληθής, ες, true, truthful:

	Masculine and Feminine			**Neuter**	
	Singular	**Plural**		**Singular**	**Plural**
N.	ἀληθ_____	ἀληθ_____		ἀληθ_____	ἀληθ_____
G.	ἀληθ_____	ἀληθ_____		ἀληθ_____	ἀληθ_____
D.	ἀληθ_____	ἀληθ_____		ἀληθ_____	ἀληθ_____
A.	ἀληθ_____	ἀληθ_____		ἀληθ_____	ἀληθ_____
V.	ἀληθ_____	ἀληθ_____		ἀληθ_____	ἀληθ_____

3. Second Group. These have a stem ending in -_____. Fill in the endings.

	Masculine and Feminine			**Neuter**	
	Singular	**Plural**		**Singular**	**Plural**
N.V.	ἄφρ_____	ἄφρο_____		ἄφρ_____	ἄφρο_____
G.	ἄφρο_____	ἀφρό_____		ἄφρο_____	ἀφρό_____
D.	ἄφρο_____	ἄφρο_____		ἄφρο_____	ἄφρο_____
A.	ἄφρο_____	ἄφρο_____		ἄφρο_____	ἄφρο_____

4. Third Group. This is the miscellaneous group:

(i) πᾶς, πᾶσα, πᾶν. This adjective can be used in the following ways:

(a) Without the article, it means _____ (singular) and _____ (plural). πᾶς ἄνθρωπος: _____ man, πᾶσιν ἀνθρώποις: _____ men. The noun qualified by this adjective may be implied: πάντες ἥμαρτον (_____ _____ _____).

(b) With the article, as a rule it means _____ (singular) _____ and _____ (plural). πᾶσα ἡ πόλις: ___ _____ city, πᾶσαι αἱ πόλεις: _____ the cities.

(ii) ἅπας, ἅπασα, ἅπαν is the _____ form of πᾶς.

(iii) εὐθύς, εὐθεῖα, εὐθύ (straight). The masculine is declined irregularly according to the _____ declension. In the NT it is found only in the feminine in the _____ and _____ singular, and _____ plural (εὐθεῖα, _____[s], _____[pl]).

Like εὐθύς, the adjective πραΰς (masc.) πραεῖα (fem.), πραΰ (neu.) meaning "meek," is only found in the NT only in the _____masculine singular (πραΰς), the _____ neuter singular (πραέως, and in the nominative _____ plural πραεῖς. The Textus Receptus uses the word πρᾷος (nom. masc. sing.) in Matthew 11:29, and πραέος in 1 Peter 3:4.

Feminine adjectives which are declined follow the _____ declension. The masculine follows the _____, have the α of the ending in the nominative and accusative _____ short; hence the circumflex on εὐθεῖα.

(iv) Two other adjectives _____ ("great"), and _____ ("much") have already been dealt with in (16 § 12).

5. Comparison of Adjectives. The adjectives of the first group form the comparative and superlative degrees by adding to the stem certain endings. The endings give us the distinction of the degree of comparison (e.g. true; true + er; tru + est). Give the basic Greek endings of the three genders -_____, -___, -__ (comparative) and -_____, -___, -__ (superlative):

ἀληθέσ _____, -___, -_____ ; ἀληθέσ _____, -___, -_____.

Give the positive for the following forms:

_____, ἐλάσσ(ττ) ων, ον and μικρότερος, α, ον

_____, ἐλάχιστος, η, ον

_____, κράτιστος, η, ον

_____, κρείσσ(ττ) ων, ον

_____, μείζων, ον, or μέγιστος, η, ον

_____, πλεῖστος, η, ον

_____, πλείων, ον or πλέον

_____, χείρων, ον

The Interrogative Pronoun
The Indefinite Pronoun
The Indefinite-Relative Pronoun
The Noun: The Cases Indicating Time and Space

1. The Interrogative Pronoun. τίς, τί means _____? and _____? It preserves the accent on one-syllable forms, and the acute accent (turns/never turns) into the grave accent. Finish the declension with accents:

	Masculine and Feminine		**Neuter**	
	Single	**Plural**	**Single**	**Plural**
N.	τίς	_____	_____	_____
G.	_____	_____	_____	_____
D.	_____	_____	_____	_____
A.	_____	_____	_____	_____

The _____ pronoun also introduces an _____ question.

2. The interrogative pronoun τί in the _____ _____singular, by itself, or preceded by the preposition ____, is also used in the sense of _____(?).

3. The Indefinite Pronoun. To form this pronoun (which in English means, *a certain*, *some*, or similar expressions), the accent (if it has one) is kept on the _____. Usually it (follows/precedes) the noun it qualifies.

4. The indefinite pronoun is an _____. διδάσκαλοί τινες. (Note accenting. See rules, **10 § 9**).

6. The Indefinite-Relative Pronoun. It may mean _____, _____. It is formed by a combination of the _____ and _____ pronouns: ὅστις, ἥτις, ὅ τι. Note that the neuter has the two pronouns separated by a _____ to distinguish it from ὅτι: "_____," "_____."

7. Use of the Cases to Indicate Time or Space.

(i) Time.
(a) The accusative expresses the _____ of time.
(b) The genitive indicates time _____ which an event takes place.
(c) The dative indicates a particular _____ ___ time at which an event takes place.

(ii) Space.

The accusative is used to indicate the _____ of space or _____.

Lesson 31

Infinitives in All Voices
Articular Infinitive
Impersonal Verbs
Indirect Speech
The Verbs δύναμαι and γίνομαι

1. The Infinitive. The participle is a verbal _____. The infinitive is a verbal _____. It expresses a general (_____) concept of action or state. It is not linked with a _____ person: "e.g. ___ ____ is human."

2. The infinitive has _____ and _____. It (may/may not) have a subject or object. "ἐκέλευσεν αὐτοὺς ἄγειν τὸν τυφλὸν πρὸς αὐτόν": he commanded that *(they)* should <u>lead</u> <u>the</u> <u>blind</u> <u>man</u> to him. Here _____ is the subject of the infinitive ἄγειν, and _____ is the object of the infinitive ἄγειν.

"ἐκέλευσε τὸν τυφλὸν ἄγεσθαι πρὸς αὐτόν": *he commanded that <u>the blind man should be led</u> to him.* Here _____ is the subject of the infinitive ἄγεσθαι.

The subject of the infinitive is always in the _____ case.

3. As a *noun* the infinitive (can/cannot) be the subject or object of another verb. "ἔξεστιν τῷ σαββάτῳ θεραπεῦσαι": *Is it lawful ___ _____ on the Sabbath?* θεραπεῦσαι is the _____ of the verb ἔξεστιν.

"βασιλεῖς ἠθέλησαν ἰδεῖν ἃ ὑμεῖς βλέπετε": *Kings have desired to see that which you see.* . . . ἰδεῖν is the _____ of the verb _____. ἃ ὑμεῖς βλέπετε, is a _____ _____ and the _____ of the infinitive ἰδεῖν.

4. To form an infinitive the endings are added to the verb. Using the verb stem λύ and the proper ending, give the Greek for the following:

Present Active: _____
Present Middle & Passive: _____
Future Active: _____
Future Middle: _____
Future Passive: _____
First Aorist Active: _____
First Aorist Middle: _____
First Aorist Passive: _____
Perfect Active: _____
Perfect Middle & Passive: _____

The second aorist is formed by adding to the verbal stem _____, active; _____, middle; _____, passive.

91

Complete the following with accents, giving close attention to the stem: Aorist infinitive for βάλλω βαλ____, βαλ_____, βλη_____.

The second perfect active is formed by adding _____ to the reduplicated stem:

γράφω—_____.

5. Give the infinitive of εἰμί: present, _____; future, _____.

6. The infinitive is negated by means of ____.

7. The chart of irregular or (nasal/liquid) verbs found in the NT should be read aloud (across the page) until the patterns become very familiar.

8. The infinitive denotes no real element of _____ as in the finite indicative verb. The present infinitive is generally used because it (does not suggest/suggests) continued or repeated action.

9. The Noun Uses of the Infinitive. As a noun, the infinitive may take an article in the _____ gender.

(i) As a subject, particularly with the impersonal verbs _____ *(it is lawful)* and _____ it is necessary.

(ii) As a direct object, particularly with the verb _____, *(I begin)*, and with verbs of _____ like βούλομαι and _____, or of _____ like κελεύω and παραγγέλλω.

(iii) As the object of a _____.

The infinitive (cannot/can) be declined, but the article is declined in the gender required by the particular _____ used.

10. The Adjective and Complementary Uses of the Infinitive. The infinitive in both English and Greek can modify a certain verb, noun, or adjective by explaining in what way one is able or _____. _____, *(I am able)*, for example followed by the infinitive explains what "I am able to do." Nouns like _____ (authority or power), adjectives like _____ *(able)*, and _____ *(worthy)* are also used. The infinitive usually follows the verb _____ (I am about to) to complete the idea.

11. The Adverbial Use of the Infinitive. This construction is used to:

(i) Define the relationship between the infinitive and main verb in terms of time.

(a) Antecedent time: before the time of the main verb with _____ _____.

(b) Contemporaneous time: _____ the time of the main verb *while* with ____ ____.

(c) Subsequent time: _____ the time of the main verb with ____ _____.

(ii) To emphasize the _____ or aim of the action denoted by the <u>main</u> verb. There are three primary constructions with the infinitive to show purpose:

        (a) the _____ infinitive by itself.
        (b) the infinitive with the neuter article _____.
        (c) the infinitive with the preparation (and neuter article) ____ ____ or ____ ____.

(iii) To give the cause of the action of the main verb, used with ____ ____.

Some combinations in the NT are (preposition+article+infinitive):

(i) **Time**. The following constructions which denote the action of the main verb takes place in a time element that is denoted by the infinitive. Complete the following for the present infinitive of ἔρχομαι and give translation:

        (a) πρὸ + article + infinitive = _____ . . .
        (b) ἐν + article + infinitive = _____ . . .
        (c) μετὰ +article + infinitive = _____ . . .

(ii) **Purpose**. The articular infinitive:

        (a) τοῦ (genitive) + infinitive = ____ ___ _____ . . .
        (b) εἰς or πρὸς+article+infinitive = _____ . . .

(iii) **Reason**.

        διὰ + article + infinitive = _____ . . .

12. Impersonal Verbs. Impersonal verbs are employed only in the _____ _____ singular, and seemingly do not have a _____. Give translations for the most common: δεῖ ____ ____ _____, ἔξεστι, ___ _____ _____ μέλει, _____ _____, δοκεῖ _____ _____.

13. Indirect Speech. We have seen in **(18 § 9)** that ὅτι may be used to introduce an indirect _____. Indirect speech can also be used by putting the dependent clause in the _____: "πῶς λέγουσι τὸν Χριστὸν εἶναι Δαυὶδ υἱόν": *How do they say (that) Christ _____ the son of David?*

14. The Verbs δύναμαι, γίνομαι. These are _____ verbs (middle or passive in form, active in meaning): Complete the following paradigms with accents:

Present Indicative of δύναμαι:

Present		Imperfect	
Single	**Plural**	**Single**	**Plural**
δύνα_____	δυνά_____	_δυνά_____	_δυνά_____
δύνα_____	δύνα_____	_δύν_____	_δύνα_____
or δύνῃ			
δύνα_____	δύνα_____	_δύνα_____	_δύνα_____

Future		**Aorist Passive**	
Single	**Plural**	**Single**	**Plural**
δυν_____	δυν_____	__δυν_____	__δυν_____
δυν_____	δυν_____	__δυν_____	__δυν_____
δυν_____	δυν_____	__δυν_____	__δυν_____

γίνομαι.

Present		**Future**	
Single	**Plural**	**Single**	**Plural**
γίνο_____	γιν_____	γενήσομαι	γεν_____
γίν_____	γίν_____	γεν_____	γεν_____
γίν_____	γίν_____	γεν_____	γεν_____

Second Aorist		**Aorist Passive**	
Single	**Plural**	**Single**	**Plural**
ἐγενόμην	__γεν_____	ἐγενήθην	__γεν_____
__γεν_____	__γεν_____	__γεν_____	__γεν_____
__γεν_____	__γεν_____	__γεν_____	__γεν_____

Perfect		**Perfect Passive**	
Single	**Plural**	**Single**	**Plural**
γέγονα	γεγ_____	γεγένημαι	γεγ_____
γέγ_____	γεγ_____		γεγ_____
γέγ_____	γέγ_____		
γέγ_____	or γέγ_____		

γίνομαι (*I become*), may also mean: *to happen, to appear, to be made,* etc.

καὶ ἐγένετο in the KJV means _____ ___ _____ _____ _____.

καὶ ἐγένετο is often left _____ in some modern versions of the NT.

Lesson 32

The Verb: The Subjunctive
Conditional Statements
The Particle ἄν

1. The Subjunctive: Its Formation. The sign of the subjunctive is a _____ initial vowel for the ending, with ε lengthening to ___, and ο and ου lengthening to ___. The ι in the diphthongs ει and ῃ show up under the η as ____. Complete the following:

Present Active		Present Middle & Passive	
λύ____	λύ_____	λύ_____	λυ_____
λύ____	λύ_____	λύ_____	λύ_____
λύ____	λύ_____(ν)	λύ_____	λύ_____

2. The first aorist is formed by inserting the ___ between the stem and the ending. Complete the following:

First Aorist Active		First Aorist Middle	
λύ____	λύ____	λύ_____	λυ_____
λύ____	λύ____	λύ_____	λύ_____
λύ____	λύ____	λύ_____	λύ_____

3. The second aorist is formed by adding the _____ endings to the _____ stem. Complete the following with accents:

Second	Aorist Active	Second Aorist	Middle
βάλ____	βάλ____	βάλ____	βαλ_____
βάλ____	βάλ____	βάλ____	βάλ_____
βάλ____	βάλ____ (ν)	βάλ____	βάλ_____

4. The aorist passive is formed by inserting _____ between the stem and endings of the present active. Notice the accent, the ε of the aorist passive suffix combines with the ending and produces a _____ accent on ____ forms. Complete the following with accent:

Aorist Passive		Second Aorist Passive	
λυ_____	λυ_____	γραφ____	γραφ____
λυ_____	λυ_____	γραφ____	γραφ____
λυ_____	λυ_____	γραφ____	γραφ____ (ν)

95

5. Give the present tense verb with accents for the following irregular second aorist subjunctives:

-βαίνω

-βῶ	-β_____
-β____	-β____
-β____	-β____

γινώσκο

γν____	γν_____
γν____	γν____
γν____	γν____
or γνοῖ	

Other 2nd aorist subjunctives are built regularly upon the _____ aorist stem. Complete the following with accents:

ἀποθνήσκω: _____

ἔρχομαι: _____

λέγω: _____

ὁράω and βλέπω: _____

6. The present subjunctive of εἰμὶ are just the endings of the present active: Complete the following with accents:

ὦ _____

_____ _____

_____ _____

The subjunctive of οἶδα is _____.

7. The rules of contraction governing the contract verbs apply in this mood also. The subjunctive of τιμάω is τιμῶ. The contract verbs of the _____ group present a possibility of confusion, between any form of the _____ indicative and the "_____ subjunctive."

8. Generally in the NT the subjunctive is found in the present and the _____ tenses.

9. With regard to the element of time, the same rule applies in the subjunctive as in the infinitive. The _____ is used to show _____ or repeated action. The _____ is used if this action is not implied.

10. The Subjunctive: Its Role. The indicative makes _____ statements, while _____ is involved in the subjunctive. It is mainly used to introduce the "_____" (dependent) clause and completes the statement made by the main verb.

11. The Subjunctive of the "Final Clause." This usage expresses _____, and, as a rule, is preceded by ἵνα or ὅπως. So ἵνα (or ὅπως) + an infinitive should be translated as ___ _____ _____, ___ _____. The negative is formed by ἵνα . . . μὴ: and should be translated as ___ _____ . . . _____.

12. The Subjunctive of the "Indefinite Clause." The particle ἄν or ἐάν is used as the element of _____. With "ever" being added to the proper word: _____, _____, etc. εἰς ἣν δ᾽ ἂν εἰσέλθητε οἰκίαν: "____ ____ _____ _____ ____ _____." The particle _____ combined with ὅτε produces _____: whenever.

13. The "Deliberative" Subjunctive. This is used in questions if the answer is not _____ or with the intent to provoke a _____ _____: "τὶ οὖν ποιήσωμεν": *What then _____ ____ ____?* or "τὶ οὖν . . .": *What _____?* . . . *Should we sin because we are not under law?*

14. The "Hortatory" Subjunctive. The subjunctive is used in the first person _____ as an _____. ποιήσωμεν τρεῖς σκηνάς: ____ ____ _____ *three booths.*

15. The Subjunctive of "Strong Denial." Both negatives (_____ and _____) are used before the aorist subjunctive: "τὸν ἐρχόμενον πρὸς ἐμὲ οὐ μὴ ἐκβάλω ἔξω": *Him who comes to me I _____ _____ ____ _____ cast out.* Usually the subjunctive is negated by _____.

16. Conditional Statements. A conditional statement depends on the _____ of some other _____ or situation. It generally consists of ____ parts (clauses): (i) the "protasis" or the "____ clause," and (ii) the "conclusion" or "_____ clause," i.e., "____ *you believe, you will be saved.*" Conditional statements can be divided into three groups:

(i) The "protasis" refers to a (present/past/both present and past) or _____ event. The verb of the "protasis" in the _____ mood is preceded by _____. "___ δὲ πνεύματι ἄγεσθε, (dependent clause) οὐκ ἔστε ὑπὸ νόμον" (independent clause – apodosis): *But _____ ____ ____ _____ according to the Spirit, you are not under (the) law.* Here the if clause is assumed to be _____.

(ii) The "protasis" refers to a _____ event. ἐάν (εἰ + ἄν) + the subjunctive mood is used in the "protasis." "_____ τις φάγῃ ἐκ τούτου τοῦ ἄρτου, ζήσει εἰς τὸν αἰῶνα": *If anyone _____ of this bread, he _____ _____ forever.*

(iii) The "protasis" refers to an event that ____ ____ _____ and the "_____" states what might have been fulfilled if the protasis had been true. In the "protasis" the order is ____ plus a (present/past) tense of the _____ mood and in the "apodosis" it is ἄν plus (present/past) tense of the _____ mood: "εἰ ὁ θεὸς πατὴρ ἡμῶν ἦν, ἠγαπᾶτε ἂν ἐμέ." = ___ *God _____ your Father, you _____ me.*

17. The Particle ἄν. This introduces an element of _____ or uncertainty into a sentence. καὶ + ἄν = _____, when used with its verb in the _____ mood, means *if only*, or *at least*. "ἐὰν ἄψωμαι _____ τῶν ἱματίων αὐτοῦ σωθήσομαι": _____ _____ *I touch his garments, I shall be saved.*

Lesson 33

The Imperative Mood
Prohibitions
The Reflexive Pronoun
The Reciprocal Pronoun

1. The Imperative Mood. This mood gives a _____, or expresses a _____. Only the _____ and _____ persons are used in the singular and plural. The closest thing in our language to a third person imperative is a request not to stop someone else.

2. As in the infinitive and the subjunctive, the only difference between the present or aorist is the _____ of action. The present tense is for _____ or _____ action. μάνθανε: ___ _____. If the action is thought of as a _____ action, the aorist tense is used: μάθε: _____

3. The Imperative Conjugation. Complete the following with accent:

	Singular	Plural
Present Active:	λυ_____	λυ_____
	λυ_____	λυ_____
Present Middle and Passive:	λυ_____	λυ_____
	λυ_____	λυ_____
First Aorist Active:	λυ_____	λυ_____
	λυ_____	λυ_____
First Aorist Middle:	λυ_____	λυ_____
	λυ_____	λυ_____
First Aorist Passive:	λυ_____	λυ_____

4. Adding these endings to the particular stem of this tense forms the second aorist active and middle.

(i) The _____ voice endings are the same as the present active:

Give the second aorist active imperative for βάλλω and give the second aorist middle with accent:

βαλ_____ βάλ_____
βαλ_____ βαλ_____

The following have the accent on the _____: Accent these: ἐλθέ, εἰπέ.

99

One irregularity of the active second singular is the possibility of the preposition in a compound verb being accented.

Accent παρελθε.

(ii) Conjugate the second aorist middle imperative of βάλλω:

βα_____ βα_____

βα_____ βα_____

Notice the accent of the present middle drops to the _____ in the second person _____.

(iii) The second aorist passive has endings similar to the first aorist passive, the difference consisting in the ___ being dropped, and the **τ** in the second person _____ is substituted by ____. Give paradigm with accents:

στέλλω   _____   _____

_____   _____

5. Identify the present tense of the following irregular imperative forms.

βηθι- <u>aorist active imperative second person singular</u>

βάτω- _____

γενηθήτω- _____

γνώτωσαν- _____

6. Finish the present imperative of εἰμὶ (with accents):

ἴσθι   _____

ἔστω   _____

7. The imperative of contract verbs follows the regular rules. Complete the paradigm with accents:

Present Active		**Aorist Active**	
φίλ_____	φιλ_____	φίλ_____	φιλ_____
φιλ_____	φιλ_____	φιλ_____	φιλ_____

8. Prohibition. A prohibition is expressed by ___ followed by:

(i) The present imperative for a command to _____ an action already begun: (. . . μὴ κλαῖε: "_____,") or to forbid an action which is likely to be _____ or _____: ("μὴ οὖν <u>βασιλευέτω</u> ἡ ἁμαρτία . . .": **let not** *sin therefore reign . . .*).

(ii) μὴ, followed by an aorist subjunctive when there is no suggestion that an action has _____ _____. μὴ φονεύσῃς, "____ ____ _____."

9. The Reflexive Pronoun. The reflexive pronoun is used when the action of the verb refers back to the _____.

    (i) as (a/an) _____ object. "ὅστις οὖν ταπεινώσει ἑαυτὸν": *therefore* _____ *will humble* _____.

    (ii) as (a/an) _____ object "ἵνα . . . ἀγοράσωσιν ἑαυτοῖς βρώματα": *in order that . . .* _____ *may buy food for* _____.

    (iii) as an object of a _____. "ἔλεγεν γὰρ ἐν ἑαυτῇ": *for* _____ *was saying within* _____.

    (iv) as a _____. "ἄφες τοὺς ἑαυτῶν νεκρούς": let the dead bury their _____ dead.

Do not confuse the reflexive pronoun with the _____ pronoun, as in "God, himself came down."

10. The reflexive pronoun is found in (masculine/feminine/neuter/all three) (person/persons). In the neuter only in the _____ person, it is declined exactly like the personal pronoun in the 3rd person, the only difference consisting of:

    (i) In the third person, _____ is prefixed to the personal pronoun. _____αὐτοῦ, _____αὐτῆς: *of himself, of herself.* Sometimes in the third person singular the _____ is omitted, thus _____.

    (ii) In the first person singular, _____ is prefixed to the personal pronoun— _____αὐτοῦ, _____αὐτῆς: *of myself, to myself,* etc.

    (iii) In the second person singular, ___ is prefixed to the pronoun. ___αὐτοῦ, ___αὐτῆς, of thyself.

Complete ἑαυτοῦ with accent:

	Third Person	**First Person**	**Second Person**
Masc.	_____	_____	_____
Fem.	_____	_____	_____

    (iv) The plural for all three persons is identical to the pattern of the _____ person. Because it is always used as an object, there is no _____ case or _____ case.

11. The Reciprocal Pronoun means _____ _____, and is found only in the masculine gender (singular/plural). Give the forms with proper accents:

        G. _____
        D. _____
        A. _____

The plural of the _____ pronoun may be used instead of the reciprocal.

Lesson 34

The Adverb: Comparison of the Adverb

1. The Adverb. This part of speech usually modifies (a/an) _____. Less frequently it qualifies an _____ or _____. All adverbs are (declined/indeclinable).

2. Many adverbs are derived from adjectives or other parts of speech by adding the adverbial suffix ____ to the stem. καλὸς: *good*, (καλῶν) _____, ἀληθὴς: *true*, (ἀληθῶν) _____. The adjective in the neuter (_____ _____) is used in a few cases as an adverb – πολὺ: *much, greatly*; μόνον: *only*, etc.

3. Adverbs can be classified into _____ main groups and these indicate (i) _____, (ii) _____ and (iii) _____.

Adverbs of Place have endings mostly in ____ or _____. Others have endings in ___ and ____. Nouns affected by an adverb of place are put in the _____ case.

Adverbs Ending in _____ are adverbs of time.

Adverbs of Manner. Most adverbs ending in ____ are adverbs of manner.

STUDY CAREFULLY. Be sure to fill in the Vocabulary List (Adverbs) in the back of the Workbook.

The Hebrew verbal adjective transliterated into Greek as ἀμὴν is used mostly in the NT as an adverb meaning _____.

4. Comparison of the Adverb. As a rule, only adverbs derived from adjectives can have comparative and _____ degrees. The comparative degree of the adjective in the neuter _____ _____ serves as the comparative degree of the corresponding adverb. The superlative degree of the adjective in the neuter _____ _____ serves as the superlative of the adverb. Thus:

μεγάλως— μεῖζον.
πολὺ— πλεῖον or πλέον

A few adverbs not derived from adjectives however have a comparative and / or superlative degree.

Thus ἐγγὺς _____.

103

Lesson 35

1. The Numerals. A numeral may serve the following purposes. Give the purpose for each numeral named and give example:

(i) Cardinal numerals: to indicate the _____ ____ _____, _____ _____. Examples: ____, ____.

(ii) Ordinal numerals: to indicate the _____ _____ of such persons or things. Examples: _____, _____.

(iii) Adverbial numerals: to indicate _____. Examples: _____, _____.

2. These numerals are most commonly used in the NT. (Read these through at least three times, pronouncing aloud all forms – masculine, feminine and neuter. Example: εἷς, μία, ἕν, etc. (See textbook.)

3. Of the cardinals only _____, _____, and _____ and from two hundred up are declined in all _____ genders. The others are _____ except for the cardinal δύο *(two)*, which in the dative is _____. The cardinals διακόσιοι, αι, α and upwards are declined like the _____-_____ declension adjectives. The cardinals χιλιάς, -άδος, μυριάς, -άδος are declined like the _____ declension nouns.

4. Decline the cardinals one, three and four:

	M.	F.	N.	M.	F.N.
N.	εἷς	___	___	τρεῖς	_____
G.	___	___	___	___	_____
D.	___	___	___	___	_____
A.	___	___	___	___	_____

	M. and F.	N.
N.	τέσσαρες	_____
G.	_____	_____
D.	_____	_____
A.	_____	_____

5. Both ordinals and (less frequently) cardinals may be preceded by the article.

105

Translate:

"καὶ προσελθὼν τῷ πρώτῳ εἶπεν": *and when he came* _____ _____ _____ *he said.*

"ὁ εἷς παραλημφθήσεται or ἡ μία παραλημφθήσεται": ____ ____ ____ ____ _____.

6. From the adjectives ὅσος and πόσος the corresponding adverbs _____: *(as often as)*, and _____: *(how often)* are derived.

7. οὐδείς, μηδείς and Double Negatives. The adjectives οὐδείς, οὐδεμία, οὐδέν (also οὐθείς, οὐθέν) and μηδείς, μηδεμία, μηδέν: "___ ____, _____," (used also as nouns) are declined like εἷς, etc. Οὐδείς is used with a verb in the _____ mood and μηδείς with all other moods.

In translating a Greek double negative, we must make one of the negatives a _____: "μηδενὶ μηδὲν ὀφείλετε": *Owe no man* _____.

8. Usages of μή. The particle **μή** (also _____, _____) introduces questions of _____ or implications of _____. For example, "μήτι οὗτος ἐστιν ὁ Χριστός;": _____ *this be the Christ?* It may be used after verbs expressing fear or caution and means _____. "βλέπετε μή τις ὑμᾶς πλανήσῃ": *take care* ____ _____ _____ ____ _____.

9. The Negative in Direct Questions. μή or οὐ. μή introduces questions expecting a _____ answer: μὴ σὺ μείζων εἶ τοῦ πατρὸς ἡμῶν Ἰακώβ; "____ ____ *greater than our father Jacob?*" Questions expecting a _____ answer are introduced by οὐ or οὐχί: "οὐχ οὗτός ἐστιν ὃν ζητοῦσιν ἀποκτεῖναι;": ____ ____ ____ *the one whom they seek to kill?* Remember, the particular negative to be used –**μή** or **οὐ**– is determined by the expectation of the one _____ ____ _____.

10. μὴ preceded by ____ or ____ means "except," or "unless": "_____ πρῶτον τὸν ἰσχυρὸν δήσῃ": _____ *he first binds the strong man.*

Lesson
36

The "μι" Verbs:
1. δίδωμι

1. The "μι" Verbs: General Rules. Verbs ending in ω in the first person singular form the ω group. Another group of verbs ending in "μι" in the _____ person singular of the present indicative.

2. The chief characteristics are:

(i) They differ in the _____ and, _____, indicatives and a few of the _____ and _____ forms outside the indicative. Most have a first aorist active with ___ replacing the σ in the indicative as the characteristic consonant; outside the indicative most have a _____ aorist active.

(ii) Unlike other verbs, the stem is reduplicated in the _____ and _____ of all three voices. This reduplication has the repetition of the initial consonant plus ____.

(iii) The vowel of the stem is _____ in all three persons of the _____, in the present and imperfect active, and in both numbers of other tenses similar to the _____ verbs. Thus, δίδωμι, from the stem ___; τίθημι, from the stem ____ (notice the harder dental for the reduplication); ἵστημι, from the stem _____ (the original form was _____, and the place of the ____ which was dropped was taken by the _____ breathing.).

3. The subjunctive is similar to that of the "___" verbs. There is (a/an) _____ accent on the ultima in the active _____ and on the _____ in the plurals, reflecting _____.

4. The Conjugation of the "μι" Verbs. Only the present, imperfect, and aorist are fully given.

5. The Verb δίδωμι: I give. It is one of the most common in this group. Complete the six principal parts.

δίδωμι, _____, _____, _____, _____, _____
Notice the –κα ending in the first aorist form.

6. δίδωμι in the imperfect singular is similar to that of δηλόω, a contraction taking place. Thus ἐδίδο – ον – becomes _____.

Some frequent compounds are given below. Give the translations (from the vocabulary):

ἀνταποδίδωμι _____

ἀποδίδωμι   _____

μεταδίδωμι   _____

παραδίδωμι   _____

Study this section in the textbook with the hints given in **subpoint #7,** and then complete the parsing exercises on the following pages.

PARSING EXERCISES FOR δίδωμι

After memorizing the principal parts of δίδωμι and studying carefully the paradigms in the book, parse the forms given below using the formula:

Finite Verb: Tense, Voice, Mood, Person, Number
Infinitive: Tense, Voice, Label (Inf.)
Participle: Tense, Voice, Label (Part.), Case, Gender, Number.

If a form can be middle or passive, put "Mid/Pass." If a form has two possible parsings (e.g. Indicative or Imperative), list both. Then check your answers with those given on the next page.

1. δίδοτε _____, _____, _____, _____, _____.

2. ἐδόθη _____, _____, _____, _____, _____.

3. δώσει _____, _____, _____, _____, _____.

4. ἐδίδου _____, _____, _____, _____, _____.

5. δοθῆναι _____, _____, _____, _____, _____.

6. διδόμενος _____, _____, _____, _____, _____.

7. δέδωκας _____, _____, _____, _____, _____.

8. δώσωμεν _____, _____, _____, _____, _____.

9. δέδοται _____, _____, _____, _____, _____.

10. δότω _____, _____, _____, _____, _____.

11. δοθεῖσα _____, _____, _____, _____, _____.

12. δίδοται _____, _____, _____, _____, _____.

13. δούς _____, _____, _____, _____, _____.

14. δῶμεν _____, _____, _____, _____, _____.

15. ἔδωκα _____, _____, _____, _____, _____.

ANSWERS

1. δίδοτε   Pres., Act., Ind., 2 pl.,
                  Pres., Act., Imper. 2 pl.

2. ἐδόθη   Aor., Pass., Ind., 3 s.

3. δώσει   Fut., Act., Ind., 3 s.

4. ἐδίδου   Imper., Act., Ind., 3 s.

5. δοθῆναι   Aor., Pass., Inf.

6. διδόμενος   Pres., Mid., Part., Nom., Sing., Masc.

7. δέδωκας   Perf., Act., Ind., 2 s.

8. δώσωμεν   Aor., Act., Subj., 1 pl.

9. δέδοται   Perf., Mid/Pas., Ind., 3 s.

10. δότω   Aor., Act., Imp., 3 s.

11. δοθεῖσα   Aor., Pass., Part., Sing., Fem.

12. δίδοται   Pres., Mid/Pass., Ind., 3 s.

13. δούς   Aor., Act., Part., Nom., Sing., Masc.

14. δῶμεν   Aor., Act., Subj., 1 pl.

15. ἔδωκα   Aor., Act., Ind., 1 s.

Lesson 37

1. The Verb ἵημι, "to send" is found in the NT in compound forms only. It has a verbal stem of _____. The reduplication for the present and _____ tenses is _____. The most important compound verb from ἵημι is _____; and the other significant verb is _____.

2. The Verb ἀφίημι. The word has the preposition ἀπο prefixed to the stem. ἀπο + ἵημι with the elision becomes ἀφίημι. Write the definitions of:

ἀφίημι   I leave _____ _____,   ___ forgive
___ permit, I _____ _____

Give the six principal parts of ἀφίημι:

ἀφίημι, _____, _____, _____, _____, _____

5. The Verb συνίημι. This verb occurs only in the active voice of the present, _____ and _____ tenses. Give those principal parts:

συνίημι, _____, _____.

All the forms appearing in the Greek NT are identical to their counterparts given but one: The present active indicative, 3p, uses the –ασι(ν) ending, which is more typical of other –μι verbs: Thus: συν_____.

Study the paradigms in the textbook and the hints in **§ 4** carefully and then parse the following forms:

Parsing Exercises for αφίημι

After memorizing the principal parts of ἀφίημι and studying carefully the paradigms in the book, parse the forms given below using the formula:

Finite Verb: Tense, Voice, Mood, Person, Number
Infinitive: Tense, Voice, Label (Inf.)
Participle: Tense, Voice, Label (Part.), Case, Number, Gender

If a form can be middle or passive, put "Mid/Pass." If a form has two possible parsings (e.g. Indicative or Imperative), list both. Then check your answers with those given on the next page.

1. ἀφῆκε   _____, _____, _____, _____, _____.

2. ἀφῶμεν   _____, _____, _____, _____, _____.

3. ἀφεῖς   _____, _____, _____, _____, _____.

4. ἀφιέτω   _____, _____, _____, _____, _____.

5. ἀφέθη   _____, _____, _____, _____, _____.

6. ἤφιε   _____, _____, _____, _____, _____.

7. ἀφῶμεν   _____, _____, _____, _____, _____.

8. ἀφήκατε   _____, _____, _____, _____, _____.

9. ἀφιέναι   _____, _____, _____, _____, _____.

10. ἀφέωνται   _____, _____, _____, _____, _____.

11. ἀφίεμεν   _____, _____, _____, _____, _____.

12. ἀφεθήσονται _____, _____, _____, _____, _____.

13. ἀφίουσι   _____, _____, _____, _____, _____.

14. ἀφήσουσι   _____, _____, _____, _____, _____.

15. ἀφέωτες   _____, _____, _____, _____, _____.

Answers for the Parsing Exercises for αφίημι

1. ἀφῆκε — Aor., Act., Ind., 3 s.
2. ἀφῶμεν — Aor., Act., Subj., 1 p.
3. ἀφεῖς — Pres., Act., Ind., 2 s.
4. ἀφιέτω — Pres., Act., Imper. 3 s.
5. ἀφέθη — Aor., Pass., Subj., 3 s.
6. ἤφιε — Imperf., Act., Ind., 3 s.
7. ἀφῶμεν — Aor., Act., Subj., 1 p.
8. ἀφήκατε — Aor., Act., Ind., 2 p.
9. ἀφιέναι — Pres., Act. Inf.
10. ἀφέωνται — Perf., Mid/Pass., 3 p.
11. ἀφίεμεν — Pres., Act., Ind., 1 p.
12. ἀφεθήσονται — Fut., Pass., Ind., 3 p.
13. ἀφίουσι — Pres., Act., Ind., 3 p.
14. ἀφήσουσι — Fut., Act., Ind., 3 p.
15. ἀφέωτες — Aor., Act., Part., Nom., Pl. Masc.

Lesson 38

The "μι" Verbs:
3. τίθημι

1. The Principal Parts of τίθημι. The verb τίθημι: *I place, I lay,* is built on the stem _____. It is similar to ἵημι. Complete the six principal parts:

τίθημι, _____, _____, _____, _____, _____.

2. The Conjugation of τίθημι. Notice the lack of connecting vowels in the _____ and _____ voices of the _____, and _____, tenses. The endings are added directly to the ____ stem. The aorist passive presents a special problem in that the **θ** is not a part of the _____, but is the suffix ___ of the aorist passive. The reduplication is like the perfect tense where the initial **θ** of the stem is changed to the hard dental ____. Analyze the aorist passive ἐτέθην. Augment: ___; stem: ____; aorist passive suffix: ____; active ending of a lengthened vowel: ___.

Study the paradigms and the hints in **§ 3** and then parse the forms on the following page.

PARSING EXERCISES FOR τίθημι

After memorizing the principal parts of τίθημι and studying carefully the paradigms in the book, parse the forms given below using the formula:

Finite Verb: Tense, Voice, Mood, Person, Number
Infinitive: Tense, Voice, Label (Inf.)
Participle: Tense, Voice, Label (Part.), Case, Number, Gender

If a form can be middle or passive, put "Mid/Pass." If a form has two possible parsings (e.g. Indicative or Imperative), list both. Then check your answers with those given on the next page.

1. ἔθηκας   _____, _____, _____, _____, _____.

2. τίθησι   _____, _____, _____, _____, _____.

3. ἐτέθην   _____, _____, _____, _____, _____.

4. θέτε   _____, _____, _____, _____, _____.

5. ἐτίθην   _____, _____, _____, _____, _____.

6. τιθέναι   _____, _____, _____, _____, _____.

7. τεθέντος   _____, _____, _____, _____, _____.

8. θέσθωσαν   _____, _____, _____, _____, _____.

9. ἐτίθεντο   _____, _____, _____, _____, _____.

10. τιθώμεθα   _____, _____, _____, _____, _____.

11. τέθεικε   _____, _____, _____, _____, _____.

12. τίθεικε   _____, _____, _____, _____, _____.

13. θῶ   _____, _____, _____, _____, _____.

14. ἐτίθει   _____, _____, _____, _____, _____.

15. τίθεσθαι   _____, _____, _____, _____, _____.

Answers for the Parsing Exercises for τίθημι

1. ἔθηκας   Aor., Act., Ind., 2 s.

2. τίθησι   Pres., Act., Ind., 3 s.

3. ἐτέθην   Aor., Pass., Ind., 3 s.

4. θέτε   Aor., Act., Imper., 2 pl.

5. ἐτίθην   Imperf., Act., Ind., 1 s.

6. τιθέναι   Pres., Act., Inf.

7. τεθέντος   Aor., Pass., Part., Gen., Sing., Masc.

8. θέσθωσαν   Aor., Mid., Imper., 3 pl.

9. ἐτίθεντο   Aor., Imperf., Mid/Pass., Ind., 3 pl.

10. τιθώμεθα   Pres., Mid/Pass., Subj., 1 pl.

11. τέθεικε   Perf., Act., Ind., 3 s.

12. τίθεικε   Pres., Mid/Pass., Ind., 2 pl.
                 Pres., Mid/Pass., Imper., 2 pl.

13. θῶ   Aor., Act., Subj., 1 s.

14. ἐτίθει   Perf., Mid/Pass., Ind., 3 s.

15. τίθεσθαι   Pres., Mid/Pass., Inf.

Lesson 39

1. Distinctive Features of ἵστημι. ἵστημι in the present active, _____ _____, and _____ aorist in the active voice has a _____ meaning. In all other voices, it has an _____ meaning. The transitive meaning is: _____ _____, _____, and _____. The intransitive meaning is: _____.

2. The Principal Parts of ἵστημι. Complete the six principal parts:

ἵστημι, _____, _____ or _____, _____, _____, _____.

Unlike the other "μι" verbs ἵστημι has both a _____ and _____ aorist form in ____ moods. This is caused by it having both a _____ meaning and a _____ meaning.

Notice also that, unlike the other "μι" verbs, the ____ aorist has the ____ endings rather than the κα endings.

3. As with the verb οἶδα (**27 § 15**), ἕστηκα, the _____ of ἵστημι, has a present time meaning, ____ _____, rather than a perfect meaning, ____ ____ _____. Also εἱστήκειν, the _____, has a past time idea, "____ _____."

4. The present indicative participle and infinitive may be found in the form of _____. It is conjugated as the ___ verb.

PARSING EXERCISES FOR ἵστημι

After memorizing the principal parts of ἵστημι and studying carefully the paradigms in the book, parse the forms given below using the formula:

Finite Verb:	Tense, Voice, Mood, Person, Number
Infinitive:	Tense, Voice, Label (Inf.)
Participle:	Tense, Voice, Label (Part.), Case, Number, Gender

For this exercise only, distinguish between 1st Aor. and 2nd Aor. for Active and Middle. If a form can be middle or passive, put "Mid/Pass." If a form has two possible parsings (e.g. Indicative or Imperative), list both. Then check your answers with those given on the next page.

1. ἔστη _____, _____, _____, _____, _____.

2. στάς _____, _____, _____, _____, _____.

3. ἵστησι _____, _____, _____, _____, _____.

4. στῆθι _____, _____, _____, _____, _____.

5. ἐστάθη _____, _____, _____, _____, _____.

6. ἵσταμαι _____, _____, _____, _____, _____.

7. σταθῆναι _____, _____, _____, _____, _____.

8. ἑστηκότων _____, _____, _____, _____, _____.

9. στήσονται _____, _____, _____, _____, _____.

10. ἔστησαν _____, _____, _____, _____, _____.

11. ἱστάναι _____, _____, _____, _____, _____.

12. στῆσαι _____, _____, _____, _____, _____.

13. ἵσταντο _____, _____, _____, _____, _____.

14. στῆσαι _____, _____, _____, _____, _____.

15. σταθέντες _____, _____, _____, _____, _____.

Answers for Parsing Exercises for ἵστημι.

1. ἔστη   2nd Aor., Act., Ind., 3 s.

2. στάς   2nd Aor., Act., Part., Sing., Masc.

3. ἵστησι   Pres., Act., Ind., 3 s.

4. στῆθι   2nd Aor., Act., Imp., 2 s.

5. ἐστάθη   Aor., Pass., Ind., 3 s.

6. ἵσταμαι   Pres., Mid/Pass., Ind., 1 s.

7. σταθῆναι   Aor., Pass., Inf.

8. ἑστηκότων   Perf., Act., Gen. Plur., Masc.

9. στήσονται   Fut., Mid., Ind., 3 pl.

10. ἔστησαν   1st Aor., Act., Ind., 3 pl.

11. ἱστάναι   Pres., Act., Inf.

12. στῆσαι   2nd Aor., Act., Inf.

13. ἵσταντο   Imperf., Mid/Pass., Ind., 3 pl.

14. στῆσαι   1st Aor., Act., Subj., 3 s.

15. σταθέντες   Aor., Pass., Part., Nom., Pl., Masc.

Lesson 40

The "μι" Verbs:
5. δείκνυμι, ἀπόλλυμι, φημί
The Optative Mood

1. δείκνυμι. *"I show."* This verb has _____ inserted between the stem δεικ and the ending in the _____ and _____ tenses, instead of the normal reduplication.

4. ἀπόλλυμι. The active form of the verb, **ἀπόλλυμι**, means __ _____, or ___ _____. The passive form means ___ _____, or ____ _____ _____.

Complete the six principal parts:

ἀπόλλυμι, _____, _____, _____, or _____, _____, _____.

6. φημί. *"I say"*; (present indicative) – is found in the NT only in the 1st and _____ singular, 3rd plural present indicative, and imperfect third singular: _____. For other tenses, _____ is used.

7. The Optative Mood. This mood expresses a _____, or may introduce _____ _____.

8. The distinguishing vowels are:

    (i) ___ in the present, and second aorist _____ and _____ voices.
    (ii) ___ for the first aorist _____ and _____ tenses.
    (iii) ___ for the aorist passive.

10. The optative is negated by the use of? _____. Translate μὴ γένοιτο: _____ (KJV = _____).

Carefully study the paradigms for δείκνυμι and ἀπόλλυμι and the hints in Lesson 40, **Subpoint 6** of the textbook, and parse the forms on the following page.

PARSING EXERCISES FOR δείκνυμι and ἀπόλλυμι.

After studying the paradigms for δείκνυμι and ἀπόλλυμι carefully, parse the forms given below using the following formula:

Finite Verb: Tense, Voice, Mood, Person, Number
Infinitive: Tense, Voice, Label (Inf.)
Participle: Tense, Voice, Label (Part.), Case, Number, Gender

If a form can be middle or passive, put "Mid/Pass." If a form has two possible parsings (e.g. Indicative or Imperative), list both. Then check your answers with those given on the next page.

1. δείξω _____, _____, _____, _____, _____.

2. ἔδειξεν _____, _____, _____, _____, _____.

3. δειχθέντα _____, _____, _____, _____, _____.

4. δεῖξον _____, _____, _____, _____, _____.

5. ἀπώλεσεν _____, _____, _____, _____, _____.

6. ἀπολλύει _____, _____, _____, _____, _____.

7. ἀπολοῦμαι _____, _____, _____, _____, _____.

8. ἀπολλύμεθα _____, _____, _____, _____, _____.

9. ἀπολωλότα _____, _____, _____, _____, _____.

10. ἀπόληται _____, _____, _____, _____, _____.

ANSWERS FOR THE PARSING EXERCISES FOR
δείχνυμι AND απόλλυμι.

1. δείξω   Fut., Act., Ind., 1 s. or
       Aor., Act., Subj., 1 s.

2. ἔδειξεν   Aor., Act., Ind., 3 s.

3. δειχθέντα Aor., Pass., Part., Acc., Sing., Masc.
       (or Nom./Acc., Pl., Neut.)

4. δεῖξον   Aor., Act., Imper., 2 s.

5. ἀπώλεσεν Aor., Act., Ind., 3 s.

6. ἀπολλύει Pres., Act., Ind., 3 s.

7. ἀπολοῦμαι Aor., Mid/Pass., 1 s.

8. ἀπολλύμεθα Pres., Mid/Pass., Ind. 1 pl.

9. ἀπολωλότα Perf., Act., Part., Nom./Acc., Neut., Pl.

10. ἀπόληται Aor., Mid., Subj., 3 s.

SECTION II

The Greek words are listed in the order that they appear in the textbook (Vocabulary) under: ADJECTIVES, ADVERBS, PREPOSITIONS, PRONOUNS, NOUNS, and VERBS.

As you study each lesson, write in the English definition of the word from the lesson. This will give you a study guide for memorizing the vocabulary. Words not listed in this section may be found in the textbook:

Pages 271-298 – GREEK/ENGLISH Vocabulary
Pages 299-322 – ENGLISH/GREEK Vocabulary

SUMMARY OF MORPHOLOGY

Examples of the declensions of Nouns, the Article, Adjectives, and the Conjugation of Verbs are given on pages 259-270 in the textbook. Get a good knowledge of the Greek language by studying this section carefully. Refer to it often as necessary. **Know where to find the answers!**

Adjectives

Chapter 7

ἀγαθός, ή, όν _____

ἀγαπητός, ή, όν _____

ἅγιος, α, ον _____

ἄδικος, ος, ον _____

αἰώνιος, ος, ον _____

ἄλλος, η, ο _____

ἁμαρτωλός, ός, όν _____

ἄπιστος, ος, ον _____

δίκαιος, α, ον _____

ἔσχατος, η, ον _____

καθαρός, ά, όν _____

καινός, ή, όν _____

καλός, ή, όν _____

μακάριος, α, ον _____

μικρός, ά, όν _____

νεκρός, ά, όν _____

νέος, α, ον _____

πιστός, ή, όν _____

πονηρός, ά, όν _____

πρεσβύτερος, α, ον _____

πρῶτος, η, ον _____

Chapter 8

ταπεινός, ή, όν _____

φίλος, η, ον _____

Chapter 9

μόνος, η, ον _____

ὀλίγος, η, ον _____

Chapter 10

ἀκάθαρτος, ος, ον _____

ἀληθινός, ή, όν _____

ἕτερος, α, ον _____

καθαρός, ά, όν _____

ὅλος, η, ον _____

τυφλός, ή, όν _____

Chapter 12

κενός, ή, όν _____

   fig. _____

μέσος, η, ον _____

   ἐν μέσῳ _____

   ἐκ μέσου _____

μωρός, ά, όν _____

παλαιός, ά, όν _____

σοφός, ή, όν _____

τέλειος, α, ον _____

φρόνιμος, ος, ον _____

Chapter 13

ἄξιος, α, ον _____

ἐκλεκτός, ή, όν _____

κρυπτός, ή, όν _____

λευκός, ή, όν _____

λοιπός, ή, όν _____

  τὸ λοιπόν _____

  τοῦ λοιποῦ _____

πλούσιος, α, ον _____

πτωχός, ή, όν _____

φανερός, ά, όν _____

χωλός, ή, όν _____

CHAPTER 15

ἕκαστος, η, ον _____

ἱκανός, ή, όν _____

_____

_____

ὅμοιος, α, ον _____

CHAPTER 16

ἴδιος, α, ον _____

  κατ᾽ ἰδίαν _____

μέγας, μεγάλη, μέγα _____

πολύς, πολλή, πολύ _____

CHAPTER 18

κακός, ή, όν _____

παραλυτικός, ή, όν _____

CHAPTER 19

ἐλεύθερος, α, ον _____

CHAPTER 21

ἁπλοῦς, ῆ, οῦν _____

CHAPTER 24

ἀδύνατος, ος, ον _____

CHAPTER 26

κωφός, ή, όν _____

CHAPTER 29

ἀληθής, ής, ές _____

ἅπας, ἅπασα, ἅπαν _____

ἀσθενής, ής, ές _____

ἄφρων, ων, ον _____

εὐθύς, εῖα, ές _____

ἰσχυρός, ά, όν _____

μονογενής, ής, ές _____

ὅσος, η, ον _____

_____

πᾶς, πᾶσα, πᾶν _____

πλήρης, ης, ες, full (with genitive),

πραΰς (also πρᾷος), εῖα, ὺ _____

_____

ὑγιής, ής, ές _____

CHAPTER 30

ταλαίπωρος, ος, ον _____

Adverbs

Chapter 8

νῦν _____

οὐκέτι _____

τότε _____

Chapter 13

ὅτε _____

Chapter 14

οὔπω _____

Chapter 17

ἤδη _____

Chapter 19

ἔξω _____

Chapter 22

ὅτε _____

Chapter 23

ὡς _____

Chapter 26

πῶς _____

Chapter 28

ἔτι _____

εὐθύς _____

Chapter 30

μεταξύ _____

_____

πότε _____

ποτέ _____

σήμερον _____

Chapter 31

καθώς _____

πάλιν _____

ὡσεί _____

ὥστε _____

Chapter 32

αὔριον _____

ἐκεῖ _____

ADVERBS OF PLACE

CHAPTER 34

ἄνω _____

ἄνωθεν _____

δεῦρο _____

δεῦτε _____

ἐγγύς _____

ἐκεῖ _____

ἐκεῖθεν _____

ἔμπροσθεν _____

ἐνθάδε _____

ἐντεῦθεν _____

ἔξω _____

ἔξωθεν _____

ἐπάνω _____

ἔσω _____

ἔσωθεν _____

κάτω _____

μακρὰν _____

μακρόθεν _____

ὅθεν _____

ὄπισθεν _____

ὀπίσω _____

ὅπου _____

οὗ _____

πανταχοῦ _____

πέραν _____

_____

πλησίον _____

πόθεν _____

ποῦ _____

ὧδε _____

ADVERBS OF TIME

CHAPTER 34

ἀεί _____

ἄρτι _____

αὔριον _____

εἶτα _____

ἐπαύριον _____

ἔπειτα _____

ἔτι _____

εὐθέως, εὐθύς _____

ἕως _____

ἤδη _____

νῦν, νυνί _____

ὅτε _____

οὐδέποτε (μηδέποτε) _____

οὐκέτι (μηκέτι) _____

οὔπω (μήπω) _____

πάλιν _____

πάντοτε _____

πολλάκις _____

πότε _____

ποτέ _____

πρωΐ _____

πώποτε _____

σήμερον _____

τότε _____

ADVERBS OF MANNER

CHAPTER 34

ἀληθῶς _____

δικαίως _____

δωρεάν _____

εὖ _____

καθώς _____

κακῶς _____

καλῶς _____

λάθρα _____

μᾶλλον _____

ὁμοίως _____

ὁμοῦ _____

ὅμως _____

ὄντως _____

οὕτως _____

παραχρῆμα _____

πῶς _____

σφόδρα _____

ταχέως _____

_____

χωρίς _____

_____

ὡς _____

The Hebrew verbal adjective transliterated into Greek as ἀμήν is used in the NT mostly as _____.

CHAPTER 35

ἅπαξ _____

δίς _____

ἑπτάκις _____

ὁσάκις _____

πεντάκις _____

ποσάκις _____

τρίς _____

Conjunctions
Numbers in Parenthesis Are Chapter Numbers Where the Words Are Found.

καί (3,6) _____

ἀλλά (6) _____

οὐδέ (6) _____

δέ (6) _____

γάρ (7) _____

οὖν (17) _____

τε (18) _____

εἰ (26) _____

ὅταν (32) _____

οὔτε . . . οὔτε
μήτε . . . μήτε (32) _____

PARTICLES

Numbers in Parenthesis Are Chapter Numbers Where the Words Are Found.

ἄν (32) _____

ἄρα (40) _____

ἐάν (32) _____

εἰ (26) _____

ἤ (13) _____

ἰδού (28) _____

μέν (6) _____

μή (6,33,35) _____

οὐ, οὐκ, ουχ (6) _____

NOUNS

CHAPTER 4

ἄγγελος, ὁ _____

ἀδελφός, ὁ _____

ἄνθρωπος, ὁ _____

ἀπόστολος, ὁ _____

διδάσκαλος, ὁ _____

δοῦλος, ὁ _____

δῶρον, τό _____

θεός, ὁ _____

ἱερόν, τό _____

κόσμος, ὁ _____

κύριος, ὁ _____

λόγος, ὁ _____

ναός, ὁ _____

ὁδός, ἡ _____

τέκνον, τό _____

Χριστός, ὁ _____

CHAPTER 5

ἀλήθεια, ἡ _____

ἁμαρτία, ἡ _____

βασιλεία, ἡ _____

γλῶσσα, ἡ _____

δόξα, ἡ _____

εἰρήνη, ἡ _____

ἐκκλησία, ἡ _____

ἐντολή, ἡ _____

ἐπιστολή, ἡ _____

ζωή, ἡ _____

ἡμέρα, ἡ _____

καρδία, ἡ _____

μαθητής, ὁ _____

Μεσσίας, ὁ _____

παραβολή, ἡ _____

προσευχή, ἡ _____

προφήτης, ὁ _____

Σατανᾶς, ὁ _____

τελώνης, ὁ _____

φωνή, ἡ _____

ὦ _____

CHAPTER 6

ἀγάπη, ἡ _____

ἄρτος, ὁ _____

γραφή, ἡ _____

ἐπαγγελία, ἡ _____

ἔργον, τό _____

θάνατος, ὁ _____

λίθος, ὁ _____

οἶκος, ὁ _____

πρόσωπον, τό _____

ψυχή, ἡ _____

ὥρα, ἡ _____

CHAPTER 8

εὐαγγέλιον, τό_____

θύρα, ἡ_____

Ἰησοῦς, ὁ_____

λεπρός, ὁ_____

πρεσβύτερος, ὁ _____

σάββατον, τό_____

συναγωγή, ἡ _____

υἱός, ὁ _____

CHAPTER 9

ἀγρός, ὁ_____

βιβλίον, τό_____

δένδρον, τό _____

ἔρημος, ἡ _____

ἐχθρός, ά, όν_____

Ἰουδαῖος, ὁ _____

καρπός, ὁ _____

ὀλίγος η, ον _____

πλοῖον, τό _____

φόβος, ὁ_____

CHAPTER 10

διάβολος, ὁ _____

θησαυρός, ὁ_____

οἶνος, ὁ _____

οὐρανός, ὁ_____

σοφία, ἡ_____

σταυρός, ὁ_____

τόπος, ὁ_____

ὑπομονή, ἡ _____

CHAPTER 11

βιβλίον _____

δαιμόνιον, τό _____

σταυρός _____

CHAPTER 12

διαθήκη, ἡ _____

διδασκαλία, ἡ _____

διδαχή, ἡ _____

δικαιοσύνη, ἡ _____

εὐλογία, ἡ _____

θρόνος, ὁ_____

θυσία, ἡ _____

κεφαλή, ἡ_____

κοινωνία, ἡ _____

κριτής, ὁ _____

μισθός, ὁ _____

μυστήριον, τό _____

νόμος, ὁ_____

πρόβατον, τό_____

CHAPTER 13

διάκονος, ὁ _____

ἐργάτης, ὁ _____

μαρτυρία, ἡ_____

μετάνοια, ἡ_____

ὑποκριτής, ὁ _____

φαρισαῖος, ὁ _____

χαρά, ἡ_____

CHAPTER 14

ἀρχή, ἡ_____

CHAPTER 15

ἐξουσία, ἡ _____

ὀφθαλμός, ὁ _____

ὄχλος, ὁ _____

σημεῖον, τό _____

CHAPTER 16

παρουσία, ἡ _____

_____

ποτήριον, τό _____

στέφανος, ὁ _____

τράπεζα, ἡ _____

CHAPTER 17

βαπτιστής, ὁ _____

ἱμάτιον, τό _____

Ἰωάννης, ὁ _____

καιρός, ὁ _____

λαός, ὁ _____

Παῦλος, ὁ _____

Πέτρος, ὁ _____

χρεία, ἡ _____

χρόνος, ὁ _____

CHAPTER 18

ἥλιος, ὁ _____

θάλασσα, ἡ _____

κώμη, ἡ _____

ὀργή, ἡ _____

παρθένος, ἡ _____

πειρασμός, ὁ _____

ποταμός, ὁ _____

σωτηρία, ἡ _____

CHAPTER 19

γάμος, ὁ _____

γενεά, ἡ _____

μνημεῖον, τό _____

νεφέλη, ἡ _____

νύμφη, ἡ _____

νυμφίος, ὁ _____

παιδίον, τό _____

τάλαντον, τό _____

τιμή, ἡ _____

φυλακή, ἡ _____

CHAPTER 22

ἄκανθα, ης, ἡ _____

δεῖπνον, τό _____

ῥίζα, ἡ _____

σκάνδαλον, τό _____

CHAPTER 23

αἰών, αἰῶνος, ὁ _____

εἰς τὸν αἰῶνα _____

εἰς τοὺς αἰῶνας τῶν αἰώνων

_____

ἀνήρ, ἀνδρός, ὁ _____

ἄρχων, ἄρχοντος, ὁ _____

ἀστήρ, ἀστέρος, ὁ _____

γυνή, γυναικός, ἡ _____

Ἕλλην, Ἕλληνος, ὁ _____

ἐλπίς, ἐλπίδος, ἡ _____

ἡγεμών, ἡγεμόνος, ὁ _____

θρίξ, τριχός, ἡ _____

θυγάτηρ, θυγατρός, ἡ _____

μάρτυς, μάρτυρος, ὁ _____

μήτηρ, μητρός, ἡ _____

νύξ, νυκτός, ἡ _____

παῖς, παιδός, ὁ, ἡ _____

πατήρ, πατρός, ὁ _____

ποιμήν, ποιμένος, ὁ _____

πούς, ποδός, ὁ _____

σάρξ, σαρκός, ὁ _____

σωτήρ, σωτῆρος, ὁ _____

χάρις, χάριτος, ἡ _____

χείρ, χειρός, ἡ _____

CHAPTER 24

ἁλιεὺς (ἁλεεύς), ἁλιέως, ὁ _____

_____

ἀνάστασις, ἀναστάσεως, ἡ

_____

ἀποκάλυψις, ἀποκαλύψεως, ἡ

_____

ἀρχιερεύς, ἀρχιερέως, ὁ

_____

ἄφεσις, ἀφέσεως, ἡ _____

_____

βασιλεύς, βασιλέως, ὁ _____

γνῶσις, γνώσεως, ἡ _____

γονεύς, γονέως, ὁ _____

γραμματεύς, γραμματέως, ὁ _____

δέησις, δεήσεως, ἡ _____

δύναμις, δυνάμεως, ἡ _____

θλῖψις, θλίψεως, ἡ _____

ἱερεύς, ἱερέως, ὁ _____

ἰχθύς, ἰχθύος, ὁ _____

κρίσις, κρίσεως, ἡ _____

κτίσις, κτίσεως, ἡ _____

νοῦς, νοός, ὁ _____

παράδοσις, παραδόσεως, ἡ

_____

παράκλησις, παρακλήσεως, ἡ

_____

πίστις, πίστεως, ἡ _____

πόλις, πόλεως, ἡ _____

συνείδησις, συνειδήσεως, ἡ

_____

φύσις, φύσεως, ἡ _____

CHAPTER 25

αἷμα, αἵματος, τό _____

βάπτισμα, βαπτίσματος, τό

_____

γένος, γένους, τό _____

ἔθνος, ἔθνους, τό _____

ἔλεος, ἐλέους, τό _____

θέλημα, θελήματος, τό _____

μέλος, μέλους, τό _____

μέρος, μέρους, τό _____

ὄνομα, ὀνόματος, τό _____

ὄρος, ὄρους, τό _____

οὖς, ὠτός, τό _____

πλῆθος, πλήθους, τό _____

πνεῦμα, πνεύματος, τό _____

πῦρ, πυρός, τό _____

ῥῆμα, ῥήματος, τό _____

σκεῦος, σκεύους, τό _____

σκότος, σκότους, τό _____
 also σκοτία, ἡ

σπέρμα, σπέρματος, τό _____

στόμα, στόματος, τό _____

σῶμα, σώματος, τό _____

τέλος, τέλους, τό _____

ὕδωρ, ὕδατος, τό _____

φῶς, φωτός, τό _____

χάρισμα, χαρισματος, τό _____

_____

CHAPTER 26

Ἰερουσαλήμ, ἡ _____

Ἰεροσόλυμα, τά _____

κόπος, ὁ _____

Μωϋσῆς, ὁ _____

(-έως, -εῖ, -ῆ, -ῆν), ὁ

CHAPTER 27

Γαλιλαία, ἡ _____

πρᾶγμα, πράγματος, τό _____

_____

CHAPTER 28

Βηθλεέμ, ἡ _____

Δαυίδ, ὁ _____

Ἰουδαία, ἡ _____

κλίνη, ἡ _____

οἰκία, ἡ _____

CHAPTER 29

γῆ, ἡ _____

χήρα, ἡ _____

CHAPTER 30

εἰκών, εἰκόνος, ἡ _____

κραυγή, ἡ _____

πέτρα, ἡ _____

στρατιώτης, ὁ _____

CHAPTER 31

Ἀβραάμ, ὁ _____

ἀδελφή, ἡ _____

Ἡρῴδης, ου, ὁ _____

Ἰάκωβος, ὁ _____

κέρδος, κέρδους, τό _____

Σαδδουκαῖος, ὁ _____

CHAPTER 32

ἀσθένεια, ἡ _____

δωρεά, ἡ _____

Ἡλίας, ὁ _____

κληρονομία, ἡ _____

κληρονόμος, ὁ _____

πάσχα, τό _____

CHAPTER 34

ἑκατοντάρχης, ου, ὁ _____

CHAPTER 40

ἀργύριον, ου, τό _____

PREPOSITIONS

With the Genitive
CHAPTER 9

ἀντί _____

ἀπό _____

ἐκ _____

πρό _____

With the Dative
CHAPTER 9

ἐν _____

σύν _____

With the Accusative
CHAPTER 9

ἀνά _____

_____

εἰς _____

With Two Cases
CHAPTER 9

διά (gen.) _____

διά (acc.)

κατά (gen.) _____

κατά (acc.) _____

μετά (gen.) _____

μετά (acc.)

περί (gen.) _____

περί (acc.) _____

πρός (dat.) _____

πρός (acc.) _____

ὑπέρ (gen.) _____

ὑπέρ (acc.) _____

ὑπό (gen.) _____

ὑπό (acc.) _____

With Three Cases
CHAPTER 10

ἐπί (gen.) _____

(dat.) _____

(acc.) _____

παρά (gen.) _____

(dat.) _____

(acc.) _____

Adverbs that Also Serve as Prepositions
CHAPTER 19

ἔξω _____

CHAPTER 30

μεταξὺ _____

PRONOUNS

CHAPTER 12

ἐγώ _____

ἡμεῖς _____

αὐτός, αὐτή, αὐτὸ _____

CHAPTER 17

ὅς, ἥ, ὃ _____

CHAPTER 22

ἐμός, ἐμή, ἐμόν_____

σός, σή, σόν _____

CHAPTER 30

Complete the declension of the Interrogative Pronoun:

Masculine and Feminine   **Neuter**

Singular

N. τίς,   τί

G. _____   _____

D. _____   _____

A. _____   _____

Plural

N. τίνες,   τίνα

G. _____   _____

D. _____   _____

A. _____   _____

CHAPTER 33

The Reciprocal Pronoun

ἀλλήλων_____

The reciprocal pronoun has no nominative or vocative.

Complete the following paradigm:

Gen. ἀλλήλων

Dat. _____

Acc. _____

(Use the space below to write other pronouns.)

Verbs

Chapter 3

ἀκούω _____

βαπτίζω _____

βλέπω _____

γινώσκω _____

γράφω _____

διδάσκω _____

ἐγείρω _____

ἔχω _____

λαμβάνω _____

λέγω _____

λύω _____

μανθάνω _____

σῴζω _____

φέρω _____

Chapter 6

βάλλω _____

δοξάζω _____

ἐσθίω _____

εὑρίσκω _____

κηρύσσω _____

κρίνω _____

πέμπω _____

Chapter 8

ἁγιάζω _____

ἀνοίγω _____

δείκνύω _____

ἐλέγχω _____

_____

καθαρίζω _____

κλαίω _____

κλείω _____

νηστεύω _____

σκανδαλίζω _____

_____

χαίρω _____

Chapter 9

ἄγω _____

ἐγγίζω _____

_____

ἑτοιμάζω _____

μένω _____

πάσχω _____

πίπτω _____

σπείρω _____

φεύγω _____

Chapter 10

διώκω _____

κρύπτω _____

πίνω _____

πιστεύω _____

Chapter 11

ἀναβαίνω _____

ἀναβλέπω _____

ἀναγινώσκω_____

ἀπάγω_____

ἀποθνήσκω_____

ἀποκτείνω_____

ἀπολύω_____

ἀποστέλλω_____

βαίνω_____

ἐγκαταλείπω_____

ἐκβάλλω_____

ἐπιγινώσκω_____

ἐπιστρέφω_____

καταβαίνω_____

κατακρίνω_____

καταλείπω_____

λείπω_____

παραλαμβάνω_____

προσφέρω_____

συλλαμβάνω_____

συνάγω_____

ὑπακούω_____

ὑποστρέφω_____

ἅπτομαι_____

ἄρχομαι_____

ἄρχω_____

γεύομαι_____

γίνομαι_____

δέχομαι_____

ἐντέλλομαι_____

ἐργάζομαι_____

ἔρχομαι_____

As compound: ἔρχομαι

    ἀν(α)-_____

    ἀπ(ο)-_____

    δι(α)-_____

    εἰσ-_____

    ἐξ-_____

    κατ(α)-_____

    προσ-_____

    συν-_____

εὐαγγελίζομαι_____
_____

πορεύομαι_____

προσεύχομαι_____

Chapter 12

ἀποκαλύπτω_____

φυλάσσω_____

Chapter 13

θεραπεύω_____

Chapter 14

ἀποκρίνομαι_____

Chapter 15

ἁμαρτάνω_____

βαστάζω_____

ἐλπίζω_____

θαυμάζω_____

καθίζω_____

κράζω_____

πειράζω _____

πράσσω _____

Chapter 16

ἐκπορεύομαι _____

ἐμπαίζω _____

καλύπτω_____

πείθω _____

ταράσσω_____

τίκτω_____

Chapter 17

αἴρω _____

_____

ἀπαγγέλλω _____

βλαστάνω_____

ὑποτάσσω_____

φονεύω _____

Chapter 19

ἀσπάζομαι _____

στρέφω _____

Chapter 20

ἀγαπάω _____

αἰτέω_____

ἀκολουθέω_____

ἀρνέομαι _____

δηλόω _____

διψάω _____

ἐρωτάω_____

_____

εὐλογέω _____

ζητέω _____

θανατόω_____

καλέω _____

λαλέω _____

μαρτυρέω _____

μετανοέω _____

ὁμολογέω _____

ὁράω _____

πεινάω _____

ποιέω _____

σταυρόω _____

τηρέω _____

τιμάω _____

φανερόω _____

_____

φιλέω _____

φοβέομαι _____

Chapter 21

ἀγνοέω _____

ἀδικέω _____

ἀθετέω _____

ἀσθενέω _____

βλασφημέω_____

_____

διακονέω _____

δικαιόω _____

δοκέω _____

ἐλεέω_____

ἐλευθερόω _____

ἐπιτιμάω _____

εὐχαριστέω _____

ζάω _____

θεάομαι _____

ἰάομαι _____

κατηγορέω _____

κλάω _____

λυπέω _____

μεριμνάω _____

μισέω _____

οἰκοδομέω _____

παρακαλέω _____

_____

περιπατέω _____

πλανάω _____

ἀποπλανάω _____

πληρόω _____

προσκυνέω _____

σιωπάω _____

συντελέω _____

τελέω _____

CHAPTER 22

ἀναγγέλλω _____

_____

ἀνατέλλω _____

_____

ἐμβαίνω _____

ἐπαίρω _____

ἐπιβάλλω _____

ἐπιμένω _____

κατοικέω _____

ξηραίνω _____

_____

ποιμαίνω _____

ὑπομένω _____

φαίνω _____

CHAPTER 23

διαφέρω _____

CHAPTER 25

γεννάω _____

δουλεύω _____

CHAPTER 26

δέω _____

κοπιάω _____

κρατέω _____

CHAPTER 27

ἐπερωτάω _____

θεωρέω _____

κρούω _____

οἶδα _____

παραγγέλλω _____

πενθέω _____

πέποιθα _____

περισσεύω _____

_____

χορτάζω _____

_____

CHAPTER 28

ἐπιπίπτω _____

κάθημαι _____

ὁμοιόω _____

παραγίνομαι _____

προάγω_____

_____

ὑπάγω_____

CHAPTER 29

ἀπαιτέω _____

δουλεύω _____

ἐκκόπτω _____

κληρονομέω _____

προσδοκάω _____

CHAPTER 30

καθεύδω _____

κλέπτω _____

κοιμάομαι _____

ῥύομαι _____

ταπεινόω _____

CHAPTER 31

βούλομαι _____

δεῖ _____

δοκεῖ_____

_____

δύναμαι _____

ἐμπίπτω _____

ἔξεστι _____

ἐπάγω _____

θέλω _____

κελεύω _____

μέλει _____

_____

μέλλω _____

_____

πλουτέω _____

συνεσθίω _____

φωνέω_____

CHAPTER 32

δεῦτε _____

ἐπαινέω _____

νικάω _____

νίπτω _____

ὀφείλω _____

CHAPTER 36

ἀνταποδίδωμι _____

ἀποδίδωμι _____

δίδωμι_____

μεταδίδωμι_____

_____

παραδίδωμι _____

CHAPTER 37

ἀφίημι_____

_____

συνίημι _____

CHAPTER 38

ἀποτίθημι _____

διατίθημι _____

ἐπιτίθημι _____

_____

μετατίθημι _____

_____

παρατίθημι _____

περιτίθημι _____

προστίθημι _____

τίθημι _____

_____

ἀφίστημι _____

_____

_____

ἐξίστημι _____

_____

ἐφίστημι _____

_____

ἵστημι _____

_____

καθίστημι _____

_____

παρίστημι _____

_____

CHAPTER 39

ἀνθίστημι _____

_____

ἀνίστημι _____

ἀποκαθίστημι _____

CHAPTER 40

ἀπόλλυμι _____

_____

δείκνυμι _____

φημί _____

Numerals

	One			**Two**
	M.	**F.**	**N**	**M., F., and N**
N.	εἷς	μία	ἕν	δύο
G.	_____	_____	_____	_____
D.	_____	_____	_____	_____
A.	_____	_____	_____	_____

	Three		**Four**	
	M. and F.	**N.**	**M. and F.**	**N.**
N.	τρεῖς	τρία	τέσσαρες	τέσσαρα
G.	_____	_____	_____	_____
D.	_____	_____	_____	_____
A.	_____	_____	_____	_____

Chapter 35

δέκα _____

δεύτερος, α, ον _____

δύο _____

δώδεκα _____

εἷς, μία, ἕ_____

ἑκατόν _____

ἑπτά _____

ἔτος, ους, τό _____

κοιλία, ας, ἡ _____

μήν, μηνός, ὁ _____

ὅραμα, ατος, τό _____

πέντε_____

πρῶτος, η, ον _____

τέσσαρες, τέσσαρα _____

τεσσαράκοντα _____

τρεῖς, τρία_____

τρίτος, η, ον _____